U

REC　ı HYSELF

Uncover Satan
Recover Thyself

A Rational Satanic Recovery

BEN DEAN

All contact can be made at
ben.dean@churchofrationalsatanism.com

www.satanicrecovery.co.uk

Book design & formatting by Zesty Books
www.zestybooks.co.uk

TABLE OF CONTENTS

TABLE OF CONTENTS (CONTD.)

PREFACE

SATANISM AND RECOVERY

I am an alcoholic and I follow a 12-step recovery process as set out by Alcoholics Anonymous (AA). I have experimented with lots of other drugs but alcohol is the one that gripped and got a hold on me.

I often get asked by both confused Christians and confused Satanists as to how Satanism and recovery can work together. For me it's really quite simple and simplified further when you look at it from a rational perspective and at the science behind it.

Addiction is a physiological condition as much as it is a psychological, emotional and social issue. Alcohol especially will only be addictive in a minority of cases with people who may have a different chemical make-up in their brain. Most people will not be compelled to drink, whereas an alcoholic will no matter how much he/she drinks.

When alcohol enters my system it does not affect me the way it does a 'normal' drinker. It starts off a craving that is only stopped when my body shuts down. The increase in blood alcohol levels would 'normalise' my emotions and behaviour while also improving my functionality. By increasing my blood alcohol levels further my functionality only improves, unlike a normal drinker. This is the case until the blood alcohol level starts to drop, through me slowing down my drinking or stopping at the end of the night. I would then appear to become more and more drunk quite rapidly and people would say "I just went a bit too far and it caught up with me" or "you just had one too many again".

There came a point shortly after my 24th birthday having come around from another 7-hour black-out, on a bus, on the wrong side of town, when I felt I needed to do something about my drinking as it was having a negative effect on my life. I had attempted to deal with the situation on my own for a few years but had only been able to stop drinking for short periods. So I decided that this time I needed to get help.

I was very weary of attending AA as I had the impression it was very 'god' orientated and – don't get me wrong – it can be, the majority I have come across are Christian and Catholic. Here in the UK though I have met people of many different religious beliefs from Pagans, Chaos Magicians, Atheist and Buddhists to people who even believe the Sun is their higher power. The 12-step programme of AA is written from a Christian perspective but can easily be adapted to fit a satanic point of view with a few word adjustments.

Lots of people I see in the recovery process tend to swap their slavery of addiction to their drug of choice for an addictive slavery to an imaginary God. I see lots of people achieving milestones in recovery only to sit there and thank god for doing it for them, blaming god if it all goes wrong and I hear things like "it wasn't part of god's plan". After being a slave to my addiction for so long, I vowed never to be a slave to anything again. As a Satanist I take full responsibility for my own actions. I am the master of my own reality – no one else.

I am a Satanist and I am an alcoholic but I'm also a human, a raw, emotive, flawed animal when stripped back to my bare bones. I lost sight of myself, I stopped living for myself, I stopped living in the now, I stopped enjoying life and I allowed the compulsion to drink to take over. I therefore made a decision that I had to do something about it, I had to get back what I had so easily let slip.

Take note of all the I's and me's in those sentences, there was no flash of bright light or no angels coming down from the sky and telling me I had to stop drinking and change my ways. It was all me. When people have these delusionary visions it's because deep down in their subconscious they know that they have a problem. They however are not ready to admit it and because they can't bring this idea to their conscious, the subconscious has to create a fantasy vision, an hallucination, which can shock them into realising the truth.

When I decided to address my alcohol dependency, I no longer liked the person that was reflected back every day in the mirror. So, I took responsibility for my actions and changed from the inside out. Today I look in the mirror with pride.

I have had to search the darkest recesses of my being, through serious and honest self-examination. I have completely analysed how, what and why I reacted to situations the way I did. I have had to learn what my triggers are and how to avoid my reactions having a negative effect on my life. I had to learn the areas where I am the weakest, strengthen them or put things in place so they are not so easily exposed and exploited. I have learnt what my true strengths are and how to use them to my full advantage. Going through this process takes true strength and gave me the knowledge to understand the true power I have within. However it is an ongoing evolutionary process for me and I will learn more about myself as I face new challenges. It is also where the Futureproof Adaptability book really hit home for me.

I have gotten my alcoholism under control by not drinking. However I have to be conscious, as with any addiction, that although I have stopped feeding the initial addiction the addictive personality trait stays within me and will become attached to other things. I therefore need to focus my energy on positive things and things that can benefit me and my life. Otherwise I can be sucked into focussing on negative behaviours; feeding off negative emotions that will then become as destructive to me as drinking was. Because of this, I have utilised another aspect of my personal Satanic path and done extensive work with the rune Thurisaz.

Thurisaz is more commonly known as Thorn and many consider it a negative – or even destructive – rune. I have found though that, due to my chaotic nature, it helps me to pinpoint my focus and I use it like an expert surgeon would use a scalpel to remove unwanted growths and cancers.

The 90% 10% Thinking philosophy of Rational Satanism has been a revelation for me. It has allowed me to do things within the 10% to advance the general progress of my recovery and understand myself, where I would have stumbled before trying to find a different way of doing things. For example when people talk of god or magic, I tend to think of things rationally in terms of psychology, tricks of the mind that can be done knowingly on yourself. Lots of things start in my 10% as magic until I understand the science behind them and can implement them without the need for any kind of ritual or spell work in order for it to be successful. I do though do things in reverse sometimes and take things into the 10% for a greater effect when

I need a bit of a push in the right direction. Even though I know the science behind what I'm doing the mindset of the ritual space will give things that extra edge I might need.

I hope that, if you are struggling with any form of addiction, what you read here and the philosophy behind Rational Satanism will give you the strength to crush it, take charge and find your true power within.

Hail Thy Self

Ben Dean

"I must create a system,
or be enslaved by another man's.
I will not reason and compare:
my business is to create."

William Blake

INTRODUCTION

I do not confess to being a saint or a guru in any way shape or form, nor do I want to be. I do not hold myself in any higher regard than any other person in recovery or within any satanic circles. I do not have any fancy titles and I do not have any fancy academic qualifications. I have simply found through my years in recovery that I have a unique perspective that will hopefully help some of you to become who you were meant to be.

I'm not going to bore you with my life story or try to massage my ego by trying to write the best worst drinking story ever! I'm simply going to tell you how I used the Rational Satanism philosophy to get to where I am now.

I aim to give you, the reader, a good enough grounding of the Rational Satanism philosophy so that having to read the other books within the series is not essential. I would, however, recommend them as a follow on from this book if you find a connection with the way I have done things. It will give you a more in-depth understanding of the concepts used, allowing you to ultimately develop your own ideas and system based on your own knowledge and understanding.

This book is not designed to be a spoon-feeding exercise with a set of rules to follow; it merely provides guidelines that you can adapt to work for you. This is not a quick fix solution: it's taken me over eight years of work to get to this point, where I feel I'm able to share it. I will only be able to write about Alcoholism as that is all I know about from my own experience; however, the steps are adaptable to other addictions. You will be required to do your own research and workings to gain the best possible results. I in no way intended to write this as a self-help book; I'm just sharing with you the method I used to stay off drink.

As with all of the books in the Rational Satanism Collection[1] it is designed to give you a new perspective and a platform to work from; it is not finite or absolute. Addiction is a progressive and adaptive issue, and your recovery process should be no different.

The idea for this book sprang from the chapter I wrote for S-Theory[2] and this is now included as the preface to this edition.

Note: Language – This book is written in British English (unless in a direct quote), because, hey, I am British - born in London. So the English spelling and punctuation used are that which has evolved from the original mother tongue here in England. Sometimes, it might look unfamiliar to you if you are from outside the UK, but it would have been unnatural for me to write it any other way. I hope you will persevere because the message is worth reading. If it helps, just imagine the words spelt (spelled) the way you want them.

Note: Citation – This book covers a lot of topics, many of them factual, of which I am not an expert and have had to research. In order to acknowledge fair use of others' material, identify and give credit to authors as well as allowing you to locate them for further research, I have used a system of footnotes (endnotes) for each chapter. Within the text, you will find a superscript number which refers to a note at the end of the chapter.

Once again, I have not applied the usual placement method for superscript numbers established in most American citation systems with which you may be familiar.

I have followed an earlier British English convention, still used internationally and widely in scientific research. The footnote reference number appears after the word, title, phrase, clause or sentence, but before any punctuation marks. Hence it will be placed before the full stop (period) at the end of a sentence within a paragraph. If it appears after the final punctuation, it relates to all of the preceding paragraph or stand-alone sentence. The superscript number will also be placed after the quotation marks of a direct quote. Simple, really…

[1] The Church of Rational Satanism – The Books. (n.d.). Retrieved from http://www.churchofrationalsatanism.com/the-books/

[2] Banks, Lee. (n.d.). "Rational Satanism S-Theory by CoRS Merchandising."CoRS. Retrieved from http://corsmerch.tictail.com/product/rational-satanism-s- theory

I

LA PORTE
DE L'ENFER

La Porte de l'Enfer, or the Gates of Hell, is where you have that satanic paradigm shift, or to put it simply: a change in your perspective. It is the doorway you have to step through in order to see the AA steps from this satanic perspective: from the 3rd side. The 3rd side relates to number 3 in the 9 satanic mnemonics system, discussed below and further explained in Futureproof Adaptability[1], that we, as Rational Satanists, use to see past the face of a problem to distinguish its root course.

You will see when we look at the steps in the following chapters that I have not changed any words from the original 12 step programme; I have simply changed the way that you look at them: this is beneficial in meetings as you can use the same text as everyone else. We are going to rationally look at the steps from a satanic perspective. As you go through the book, you will hopefully see that with a pragmatic shift of the self and a new way of looking at things, you can unlock areas that were once blocked.

I have also removed the 'god' aspect from areas where I thought it was wedged into the action programmes, so you do not need to wash over them or fight against them as I did. This approach will hopefully allow you to move forward at a more comfortable pace. I have not changed the fundamental principles of the programme in any way. So if you have done this programme before and it has failed, it is because you have not been asking yourself the right questions as opposed to what you may have been told: that your answers were wrong!

Having shared this idea with other alcoholics in the rooms of AA, some of whom have a quarter of a century of atheist recovery behind them, they have been very encouraging. Many have said they wished that they had seen things from that angle from the start. I hope that you can carry this new perspective: that you learn and you adapt and apply it to your own programme. But I think, more importantly, once you recognise this paradigm shift and obtain this new perspective, you need to let others know there is a gateway to a Rational Satanic Recovery Programme.

Like most occult knowledge it is hidden in plain sight: you just need to know where to look for it within yourself. You might also be wondering why I wrote the title for this chapter in French and not English? Well, if you search for the French title, you will discover an amazing piece of artwork, which will, almost certainly, increase your understanding. An inquisitive approach while reading this book will reap dividends in the benefit you will gain from it. If things resonate with you, then you need to look further than just these pages, as you should with any text you read, to find the gems hidden in plain sight for all who choose to look.

If you have that drive to consistently know more. If you ask questions, listen, research and then formulate your own ideas and opinions based on what you have studied and then ask more questions. Then you might have the S-type personality.

Self-evolution and development are sadly not going to happen to the human race naturally, and we consider it limited to individuals that only have the S-type personality. A heightened awareness of the world and natural abilities to see things from another perspective are satanically evolved aspects that you already own, but even these can grow to personally, rationally and pragmatically better the self.

90% 10% Thinking[2] is mentioned throughout this book as it is a key part of Rational Satanism. So to help avoid confusion here is a simplified explanation of how it works:

Rational, critical and logical thinking sit firmly and make up almost the whole of the 90%. The remaining 10% is the allocated room for irrational events that you can't explain. Once you accept this paradigm, it allows you to consider moving thoughts from one part to the other. The benefit of this is that if you have difficulty understanding something in the rational 90% part, where your internal thoughts are, you could move it to the irrational 10% part, with your external thoughts which are unexplained. In this 10% part, you can work on thoughts without affecting the 90% until, if ever, you have moulded or manipulated ideas sufficiently to return to your rational side.

If you're not familiar with the other books in the Rational Satanism series, I'm now going to provide a brief description of the 9 satanic mnemonics, so that you can see how it fits in when mentioned later in this book. The mnemonics system is designed to aid memory and ease of recall.

So here are the 9 satanic mnemonics:

1   There is only one. YOU!
2   It's 2 way
3   The 3rd side
4   The 4th dimension
5   5 S's for success!
6   The 6 'R' attributes
7   The 7 steps
8   8 Satanic cognitive realms of existence
9   The 9th gate

1 THERE IS ONLY ONE. YOU!

This is you confirming you are an individual and refusing any outside influence to change who it is you are without logical evaluation.

Rational Satanism realises that there is only one where this system is concerned, the self, and that's what the system is here for: not to follow but to evolve the self to the best it can be. You need to remember it's you that's important, and it's you that you must find. Rational Satanism was designed for the self, not to follow but to adapt to a system that works for you.

2 IT'S 2 WAY

When we speak of magick, we realise it's simply intent. There are those of us who take more of a liking to the metaphysical side of greater magick, and then there are those of us who don't venture into the metaphysical and spend all our time in practical reality. 90% 10% Thinking can make the subjective objective, but it's a two-way working, one will not work without the other, it's a duality, the metaphysical won't work without the physical no matter what the intent or how strong it is.

It's not about claiming to have magickal powers or special magical titles; it's about the will of the individual. For me, this is why I incorporate Chaos Magick into my system as part of an S-theory overlap. What I tend to do is to use the 5 S's for success to look at what I want to change and what needs a push through magick. Then using the satanic 3rd side, I look into the science behind how it works and then apply it by attaching it to my will, either through ritual or sigil crafting.

3 THE 3RD SIDE

There are not two sides to every story but three. The 3rd side is where evidence is gathered, and socially gained influences are stripped out leaving the evidence and situation showing what it actually is. The Satanist could easily determine what is ultimately right from the issue by inserting logical reasoning into the problem and actually finding out the root cause.

This safeguarding third side also allows the Satanist to view all parts of the occult logically. When we look at mythology, magical orders and anything else from the realms of fantasy we look at them from the third side; this is a mental forming of pros and cons that allow us to make a pragmatic usage from our natural, logical reasoning. For me this was looking at the science behind how magick works and applying it that way.

4 THE 4TH DIMENSION

OK, so you are probably thinking astral realms or alternative dimensions where people play with mystical beings. What we, as Rational Satanists, term as the 4th dimension is the internet. It can be a great tool readily available especially in terms of mobility with smartphones but don't get sucked in and live your life on it: use it as a tool to experience the physical world around you and go outside! As you can probably tell from my tan, I get out quite a bit!

5   5 S'S FOR SUCCESS!

Kaizen (new spirit), as it was originally called on its creation in Japan, is designed to reduce waste and increase productivity on a whole. This methodical system comprises of 5 pillars, which are Sort, Set, Shine, Standardise and Sustain.

OK, so first of all, we are going to **Sort** your problems into different groups; **Set** out a priority of importance; **Shine** or clear the area by making an action plan and following it through; **Standardise** this system for all your problem solving to increase your efficiency; and try to **Sustain** it.

Simple really when it's laid out like that!

6   THE 6 'R' ATTRIBUTES

The following 6 'R' attributes are what we view to make up each and every Rational Satanist, in some form, in their own 90% (or rational %) thought process.

1. Recognition – knowing you are different with a naturally heightened sense of self.

2. Rationality – having clear thought based on reason and logic.

3. Retribution – taking vengeance on those who have wronged you.

4. Ramifications – the ability to accept and take any consequences of your actions.

5. Realist – not living in a dream world wishing for things; we go out and get them.

6. Reality – we live in the objective reality, which we carve from rational thoughts and reason.

7 THE 7 STEPS

These 7 steps are all burning in the black flame; it's the Rational Satanist's strength of mind. It's our natural perspective allowing desires, thoughts and actions to be a mirror reflection of what we see in our minds. We see these steps as a foundation to our cognition process strengthening the S-type personality and superior intuition. It's down to the individual to adapt these steps into a process and order that works for them, but with these mental foundations, it will be easy to build a solid structure.

The 7 steps are as follows:

1. Desire – Always have the desire to make something happen. Will it, not wish it.

2. Determination – fuels the black flame, never give up, drive forward towards personal success.

3. Confidence – Remember: "you will never be fully confident while you care what others think".

4. Failure – Learn from it, don't dwell on it, use the perspective we have to bounce back stronger with the safeguarding technique in place, so it doesn't happen again.

5. Resilience – Mental resilience allows us to adapt our thinking to withstand stressful situations and gains strength as we gain better thinking.

6. Pressure – Don't worry about things you can't control; that's not your problem. Craft your mental strength by acting on what you can control, so the pressure is easily handled.

7. Doubt – is a must for the satanic mind-set. Doubt is what allows us to always strive for improvement.

8   8 SATANIC COGNITIVE REALMS OF EXISTENCE

These set of tools are described in more detail in a later chapter. They are an essential part of Paradigm Shifting which, in turn, supports S- Theory.

For the sake of completeness, here is a very brief overview:

The eight realms represent an internal hierarchy, whereby the individual Satanist, by crafting their own system and not mimicking someone else's, eventually achieves the Godhead, when all the personal blocks fall into place.

The realms in ascending order are:

1. Revelation – The initial revelation of turning to Satanism is considered a realm of its own.

2. Knowledge – The knowledge we absorb is what carves out our path and our direction of thought.

3. Comprehension – All of that knowledge you've acquired you'll need to make sense of.

4. Analysis – 90% 10% Thinking concept will truly come into play to analyse and realise what you are and what works for you. You will create your own personal thinking fraction to take you further.

5. Synthesis – Essentially create a complex personal system whole by the process of combining knowledge, comprehension and analysis using dialectical reasoning based on knowledge.

6. Application – Experimentation and discovery to test out your ideas and personal understandings of practical applicability until you can begin applying your system to your objective reality.

7. Demi Godhead – In this realm you are still taking on the self-personification, but you haven't ascended to the full godhead yet.

8. Godhead – When this realm is reached you truly know the self and exactly what the self wants. You solidly have your personal fraction relating to your thought process and have attained the pragmatic maxim of applicability. This realm is yours and yours to own. It contains the large golden throne that the internal beast will sit in comfortably watching you reap the rewards that your system is bringing you.

As Satanists, we will always be on the quest for knowledge, but when the Godhead is achieved and understood, all the other realms become redundant, as all will take place in the Godhead realm. We understand ourselves to the extent that we have techniques in place that allow us to add to our personal system easily without having to wonder whether the "self" is right, we are now truly our own god.

9 THE 9TH GATE

The final satanic mnemonic, the 9th gate, is not just a great movie starring Johnny Depp!

The 9th gate represents a psychological portal that you can only open once you completely understand the self.

As we know individuality and mastery of your own world is a vital part of Satanism.

[1] Banks, Lee. (n.d.). "Rational Satanism Futureproof Adaptability by CoRS Merchandising." CoRS, Web. Retrieved from http://corsmerch.tictail.com/ product/rational-satanism- futureproof-adaptability

[2] 90% 10% Thinking. (n.d.). Retrieved from http://www. churchofrationalsatanism.com/essays/90-10- thinking/

II

THE GOD PROBLEM

Let us put to one side the idea of the Christian God for a minute. Let's go back to the first ideas and concepts of gods or spirits as the primitive human races saw them. These spirits or gods, whatever you want to call them, were based on aspects of their lives that they couldn't explain, for example; the sun, the wind, the rain and so on and so forth. Obviously, we now know what these forces are and, more importantly, they can be explained due to the advancements in scientific knowledge over the last few hundred years.

Because these mysterious influences were important to primitive man's need to survive, and they had no science to back up what was happening, they made them Gods, as in specifically named deities. These types of gods would then be worshipped and appeased in the hope of gaining the results they were after. An excellent illustration of this is the 'rain dance' performed in the hope of bringing forth rain to allow the crops to grow and provide food for the tribe.

LaVey goes on to modernise this somewhat in the Satanic Bible[1] and give God the ego aspect in the chapter 'The God you save may be yourself'. He explains that gods are simply man-made things that stem from man's own ego that he cannot deal with and so has to externalise. This mind-set, I think, came when men realised that tribes would do anything to satisfy their gods in the hope of a reward. It's at this point that I think most people get that venomous taste in their mouths.

Let's utilise both of these aspects of God and use them in a way that is useful to us as Satanists. If we take the Jung idea of shadow working[2], this combines our ego and aspects of us that we do not yet understand by making them conscious. Essentially we are using our 90% 10% Thinking[3] in its most effective way by taking the internal and making it external to be moulded and then replacing the new working model back into the internal.

So basically we are going to look at it like this: your personal symbol is Satan (or whomever you choose to use), and you sit on your throne, in your Godhead. Around you are your demigods and demons, these are the aspects of your personality that you can set forth and use once you have mastered who they are and how to use them. This place is where you will be able to explore ideas about what makes you angry or how your anger reacts in different situations; you'll learn to understand it and use it to your advantage.

So next time you see the word 'god' don't look on it with anger and taste the venom on your tongue; just smile and know that it's talking about you!

[1] ALaVey, A. S. (1969). The Satanic Bible. NY, NY: Avon Books.

[2] Jung, C. G., Campbell, J., & Hull, R. F. (1976). The Portable Jung. Harmondsworth: Penguin.

[3] 90% 10% Thinking. (n.d.). Retrieved from http://www. churchofrationalsatanism.com/essays/90-10- thinking/

III

DEFINING GOD

Let's start with a more simple definition before we delve into the more complex answers and then dissect those further.

God: the perfect and all-powerful spirit or being that is worshipped especially by Christians, Jews, and Muslims as the one who created and rules the universe.

: a spirit or being that has great power, strength, knowledge, etc., and that can affect nature and the lives of people: one of various spirits or beings worshipped in some religions.

: a person and especially a man who is greatly loved or admired.[1]

Note: It's quite clear from any study that the idea of God being perfect is a false one and any study of the

Old Testament will prove that: the great flood story being a perfect example of this.

So let us now look at the full dictionary definition. Note I have combined several definitions from different dictionaries to give the most detailed description possible.

Pronunciation: /gɒd/

NOUN

1 (In Christianity and other monotheistic religions) the creator and ruler of the universe and source of all moral authority; the supreme being.[2]

2 (god) (In certain other religions) a superhuman being or spirit worshipped as having power over nature, human fortunes or with reference to a particular attribute; a deity: a moon god, the Hindu god Vishnu.[2]

   2.1 An image, animal, or other object worshipped as divine or symbolising a god: wooden gods from the Congo.[2]

   2.2 Used as a conventional personification of fate: he dialled the number and, the gods relenting, got through at once.[2]

   2.3 (lowercase) one of the several deities, especially a male deity, presiding over some portion of worldly affairs.[3]

2.4 (often lowercase) a supreme being according to some particular conception: the god of mercy.[3]

3 (god) A greatly admired or influential person: he has little time for the fashion victims for whom he is a god.[2]

3.1 A thing accorded the supreme importance appropriate to a god: don't make money your god.[2]

4 (the gods) informal. The gallery in a theatre: they sat in the gods.[2]

5 Christian Science. The Supreme Being, understood as Life, Truth, Love, Mind, Soul, Spirit, Principle.[3]

6 (used to express disappointment, disbelief, weariness, frustration, annoyance, or the like): God, do we have to listen to this nonsense?

ORIGIN OF THE WORD GOD

Middle English, Old English; cognate with Dutch god, German Gott, Old Norse goth, Gothic guth.[3]

So before we look at the definitions in more detail here is a Bible quote:

> "Thou shalt have no other gods before me."
> *Exodus 20:3*

Taken from the King James version of the Bible implying that there are, in fact, other gods: it also claims in Exodus that he is a very jealous god.

So now we have looked at the definition of god, Christianity's own confession to there being other gods and, in the previous chapter, how primitive religions brought about the existence of god from an internal entity into an external one in an attempt to understand and make sense of it.

Delving further into this idea of god and looking at the matter from a theistic perspective: if god was ever-present, he would have to live within you; to be a part of you to some degree?

If we look at the idea of god from a subjective perspective, god will be different to different people. If god is made in our own image, then it makes hating others that look and act differently easier to do (and therefore easier to impose harsh controls on these people different to us).

If god means something different to different people, then any god has to be a personal god. Does that then not make each and every one of us our own gods: able to answer our own prayers? Are you not, as the definitions above state: able to "affect nature and the lives of people" by either your actions or your words or do you not "preside over some portion of worldly affairs"? Of course you do; you preside over your own worldly affairs; you are the ruler of your own universe, and you are in control of your thoughts and actions with the power to change them if and when you want to.

Externalisation of 'god's power' only goes so far as to explain the things that we as individuals cannot explain, as discussed in the previous chapter. However, when presented with the factual evidence to explain away the beauty and the magic of an event, it is still down to the individual to take on board this perspective.

It is also the responsibility of the person presenting the facts to understand and accept that the other individual may well be quite content with their current definition, no matter how delusional you may think it is. Just because you feel you are an 'enlightened' individual, do not go presuming that others want to be 'enlightened' also. Be content with your own conclusions and question them when necessary to further cement them, but don't expect others to be like you.

[1] God | Definition of God by Merriam-Webster. (n.d.). Retrieved from https://www.merriam webster.com/dictionary/god

[2] Realizing GOD | High Existence. (n.d.). Retrieved from http://highexistence.com/topic/realizing-god/

[3] God | Define God at Dictionary.com. (n.d.). Retrieved from http://www.dictionary.com/browse/god

IV

THE BAR PROP

You know the guy I mean: the one that sits at the end of the bar. He's there every night, same bar stool, same glass, same drink, propping up the end of the bar like some kind of structural support.

The Bar Prop is the one that talks to everyone that comes into the bar; he tells them all these elaborate ideas of what he wants to do with his life, things he wants to learn and places he wants to go. He does this at the top of his voice so the whole world can hear of the adventure he will undertake tomorrow.

The Bar Prop will always have an opinion about something that someone else has done, usually involving him having done it better or them doing it wrong altogether in the first place. He will tell you how tomorrow he will be doing X, Y and Z. Then a week later when you go see him, he's in the same spot telling someone else the same story about how tomorrow he is going to X, Y and Z.

When you speak to him and say, "I thought you were going to do that last week?" He will respond along the lines of "yeah I was gonna do that, but what happened was, something came up and I ran out of time" or some other bullshit excuse that prevented him from doing what it was he said he was going to do. You see tomorrow will never come for The Bar Prop. And so it continues, and he will forever be stuck there in this endless cycle unless he kicks away the stool himself.

Don't get me wrong: having plans and aspirations is great, and you should have those things. Just having them, though, is not enough; you need to do something about them. Not doing anything about them is like working in a toilet roll factory and complaining you don't have anything to wipe your arse with!

I see these 'Bar Prop' types constantly on the internet saying: "I want to learn things!" Well, what's stopping you? Go, learn stuff; you have a wealth of knowledge at your fingertips. When this is pointed out to them, it's normally followed up with the bullshit excuses: "but I don't know where to start!" or "I don't have money to buy lots of books!"

The answers are simple: start with something you find interesting, then you will enjoy learning it. You don't need to buy books: there is a vast array of media freely available online that you can pick from. Start with something small like an article that takes your fancy; this, in turn, will lead you to seek more things to look at as it may pose more questions. The article might not have all the information you were hoping for. You might want more than one opinion on your chosen subject. Books can also be easily obtained in pdf format now, so you don't even need to have vast amounts of money to obtain knowledge: all you need is time.

Time you have, you have a lifetime on this rock of a planet. Don't wait for tomorrow to make things happen, though, DO IT NOW! Make time to do the things you enjoy in life and things you want to achieve. If you truly want to do something, you will. You'll make the time because it will be of benefit to you; it will be something you want to do and ultimately will make you happy. Isn't that what being a Satanist is all about? Indulging in things that make you happy and are of benefit to you?

Don't be a Bar Prop: if you want to do something, just do it and talk about it after having lived the experience. Be the person that achieves something. Kick away that bar stool, stop being a Bar Prop, be a Satanist and aspire to be the best you can be.

V

12 STEPS FROM A SATANIC PERSPECTIVE

1. **We admitted we were powerless over alcohol—
    that our lives had become unmanageable.**[1]

    This one is self-explanatory: if you don't admit you
    have a problem, then you have nothing to fix!

2. **Came to believe that a Power greater than
    ourselves could restore us to sanity.**[1]

    The power greater than yourself at this stage is your
    'godhead', your archetype, your symbol of yourself,
    Satan. The reason it cannot be you at this point is
    because you do not know enough about yourself,
    despite what you might think. The sanity you are
    looking for is breaking the cycle of drinking again
    and again, and expecting different results from the
    disastrous ones you keep getting.

3. **Made a decision to turn our will and our lives over to the care of God as we understood Him.**[1]

Don't get too hung up on that G-word, because I bet you thought of a Christian god – the man with a white beard on a cloud! Now read it again from a Satanic point of view – you are making a decision to take your life back from the compulsion that drove you to have a life that you feel is unmanageable or causing you a problem. Whether by design or accident and much to the chagrin of many a born again Christian in the fellowship, the AA 'Spiritual highway' is as broad as the people in it.

4. **Made a searching and fearless moral inventory of ourselves.**[1]

This step is where you look at yourself; probe to find out who you are and what makes you tick.

5. **Admitted to God, to ourselves, and to another human being the exact nature of our wrongs.**[1]

If you can admit to yourself and, more importantly, your 'godhead' where you have been at fault, you are taking responsibility for your actions. By sharing these details with another person that may have had previous experience of the same issues, helps you to deal with them and move forward.

6. **Were entirely ready to have God remove all these defects of character.**[1]

Take your 'defects of character' and move them into your 'godhead'. I like to think of them more as aspects of my character that I wasn't able to use properly. Calling them defects of character is like someone who has never been taught how to drive complaining that the car is faulty because they keep stalling it! In the 'godhead', these no longer become issues in daily life: these defects now become tools for you to use as and when required.

7. **Humbly asked Him to remove our shortcomings.**[1]

Just because you now know how to 'drive the car' does not make you a good driver! So don't beat yourself up when you make a mistake: learn from it and work on it; store the data in your 'godhead' files, so you know for next time. Return to the 'godhead' and seek the power to manage the extremes of character just as you sought the power to eliminate the obsession to drink.

8. **Made a list of all persons we had harmed, and became willing to make amends to them all.**[1]

Along our way, through addiction and into recovery we would have done things we are not proud of and maybe unintentionally stomped on a few people. The best way to stop these things from affecting us in our daily lives is by dealing with them head on.

9. **Made direct amends to such people wherever possible, except when to do so would injure them or others.**[1]

If you know someone or something is going to cause more aggro by you going to see them or trying to fix the situation, then just let it go.

10. **Continued to take personal inventory and when we were wrong promptly admitted it.**[1]

You as an individual are constantly evolving; as a Satanist, you are constantly looking to learn new things, and your ideas will change over time; this will change how you view yourself, so it is important that you keep reviewing your own personal knowledge.

11. **Sought through prayer and meditation to improve our conscious contact with God, as we understood Him, praying only for knowledge of His will for us and the power to carry that out.**[1]

Use ritual and meditation to gain a better understanding of yourself; figure out what your goals and aims are in life; gain a focus and drive towards them.

12. **Having had a spiritual awakening as the result of these Steps, we tried to carry this message to alcoholics, and to practice these principles in all our affairs.**[1]

Use your voice to loudly and proudly say: I am a Satanist and I used these steps to get sober without your Christian God – and carry this message to other people seeking help in the fellowship who struggle with the monotheistic middle eastern death cult[2] concept of 'God'.

[1] The Twelve Steps of Alcoholics Anonymous. (n.d.). Retrieved from http://www.aa.org/assets/en_US/smf- 121_en.pdf

[2] Baddeley, G. (2016). Lucifer rising. London: Plexus Publishing Limited.

VI

SATANIC PHILOSOPHY AND ADDICTION

There has always been one key passage from the Satanic Bible[1] that has stuck with me throughout my recovery process and that is the following section from The Book of Satan IV[2]:

> Life is the great indulgence – death, the great abstinence. Therefore, make the most of life – HERE AND NOW!
>
> There is no heaven of glory bright, and no hell where sinners roast. Here and now is our day of torment! Here and now is our day of joy! Here and now is our opportunity! Choose ye this day, this hour, for no redeemer liveth!
>
> Say unto thine own heart, "I am mine own redeemer."

> Stop the way of them that would persecute
> you. Let those who devise thine undoing be
> hurled back to confusion and infamy. Let
> them be as chaff before the cyclone and after
> they have fallen rejoice in thine own salvation.
>
> Then all thy bones shall say pridefully, "Who
> is like unto me? Have I not been too strong
> for mine adversaries? Have I not delivered
> MYSELF by mine own brain and body?"

For me, this is how I felt when I was in the AA rooms. After a while, it was a "look, I'm doing this without your Christian God" attitude, and I will continue to do this as a big middle finger to him as well. Later in my recovery, I learned just to let the 'god' stuff wash over me because when people are sharing about their God, it is from their subjective views on their own recovery and not mine. Unless of course I'm being dictated to on my own recovery, then you'll see my horns!

> "The watchword of Satanism is INDULGENCE
> instead of "abstinence"...BUT – it is *not*
> "compulsion"."[3]
> *The Satanic Bible – Anton LaVey*

I also find that many of those new to the satanic philosophy and some that just don't understand the left-hand path correctly, take the indulgence aspect of Satanism and mix it in with the "do what thou wilt" approach. They think that it gives them the right to be an arsehole and continue in an entirely unproductive lifestyle.

If we look at the Nine Satanic Sins[4] of The Church of Satan, which are as follows – Stupidity, Pretentiousness, Solipsism, Self-Deceit, Herd Conformity, Lack of Perspective, Forgetfulness of Past Orthodoxies, Counterproductive Pride and Lack of Aesthetics.

You should be able to see where these will crop up in your own addiction and where these areas will try to be challenged throughout your recovery process. I'm not going to give big flashing warning signs when these are going to come into play because these may not be the same for everyone and you should be able to see for yourself.

If you take a closer look at the rational satanic perspective, there are a few things that came to my attention right off the bat. The first was the 'Life is Lemons'[5] chapter about not letting the bitterness of your past having a negative effect on your present, and this was actually what I used to base my first video[6] on for the group. The following chapter was entitled 'Save Yourself' and focuses on one's ability to truly understand ourselves with ego gratification which comprises a big part of being able to save yourself.

The most important thing for any Rational Satanist is our own vital existence, and if we are not able to indulge responsibly or are compelled to do something, then we need to be true to ourselves and do something about it.

[1] LaVey, A. S. (1969). The Satanic Bible. NY, NY: Avon Books.

[2] The Satanic Bible, Book IV – Anton Szandor LaVey. (n.d.). Retrieved from http://cparker15.tripod.com/tsb/fireIV.html

[3] The Satanic Bible, Book VIII – Anton Szandor LaVey. (n.d.). Retrieved from http://cparker15.tripod.com/tsb/airVIII.html

[4] LaVey, Anton S. (n.d.). The Nine Satanic Sins. Retrieved from http://www.churchofsatan.com/nine-satanic-sins.php

[5] Banks, Lee. (n.d.). "Rational Satanism" – Chapter – Life is Lemons by CoRS Merchandising." CoRS, Web. <http://corsmerch.tictail.com/product/rational-satanism>.

[6] Life is a lemon – YouTube . Retrieved from https://www.youtube.com/watch?v=NthR-06M7_I

VII

NOT THE ONLY WAAY

AA is not the only way to recover from addiction. I have found a successful way to do AA without relying on a Christian God, but if you find, even after reading this book, that it's not for you, that's fine. There are some alternatives and links at the end of this chapter.

> "Those unfortunates were not sicker than those who did well in a 12-step program; they were in the wrong program."
>
> – *Dr Ed Day*[1]

> "Recovery from severe addiction can come about through a variety of pathways, and is best thought of as a journey rather than an event."
>
> – *Dr Ed Day*[1]

You may find this strange to hear from someone who has found AA to work for them, but then I'm not your typical AA member, am I?

As part of my research for this book, I did a short course on addiction through King's College London. I am in no way proclaiming to be some kind of expert on addiction, though, but I thought it might be worth sharing some of the notes I took to help you find the best form of recovery for you.

> "Addiction is a complex biopsychosocial problem with a mix of intrapersonal and environmental causes. The majority of people recover from addiction without professional treatment. But in many cases, the course is prolonged, with a range of associated problems. The past 40 years has seen increasing attention paid to the study of addiction and the development of a variety of treatment approaches. However, none could be said to be the definitive answer. And so, where possible, treatment should be flexible, tailored to the individual, and open-ended."
>
> – *Dr Ed Day*[1]

I completely agree with this statement. Too many people are looking for a 'one size fits all' recovery, and this is never the case. No two drinkers are the same, so no two recovery systems should be identical. Some find the structure of meetings helpful while others will work better one-to-one or alone.

What I also come across, in my research, was a book declaring a "revolutionary alternative to Alcoholics Anonymous"[3] which claimed to be the "new cure for substance addiction" and was marketed with a commercial trademark as Rational Recovery®[4]. Obviously, with a name like that, I wasn't going to pass up on the opportunity to delve right into it.

What I was hoping to find was something along the line of a:

> "Cognitive behavioural approaches aim to reduce positive expectancies about substance use, increase self-confidence and belief in resisting drugs or alcohol, and improve skills in coping with the stresses of everyday life that might provoke a return to substance use. Patients may be taught to communicate more effectively, to be more assertive, to initiate social interaction, to respond to criticism, or to refuse offers of drugs or alcohol from others."[2]
>
> *– Dr Ed Day[1]*

What I actually found was a lot of AA bashing, regurgitation with different names, a "small book" to rival the AA big book, some wild claims and a lot of contradictions and hypocrisies.

The one I thought was very hysterical was the claim that this was the cure for substance addiction, but that addiction was not a disease. The author was dead against the idea and argued that the rational recovery process wouldn't work if you classed addiction as a disease. Personally, I believe you can, and it then leaves the option of the addiction being a disease for the scientists to prove or disprove and the individual to evaluate the evidence that best supports what they find most comforting.

However, in amongst the mess, there were a few things that struck me, and one of them was something that was similar to what I do in my own system of recovery. The focus of using the Addictive Voice Recognition Technique® (AVRT®)[5] is being in charge of your own recovery, and I can wholeheartedly agree with that part of the methodology. I have already highlighted the importance of that approach throughout this book and the importance of making a starting point in how and when to stop drinking.

> "I was solely responsible to take control and quit drinking altogether. I finally picked a time, and when that time came, I did it.
>
> Quitting for good was much easier than I thought. When I decided I would no longer drink, I resumed my life – as a person who simply does not drink alcohol. The first couple of months were the most difficult, with much yearning to drink and some irritability, but I did not become like an adolescent, as predicted by experts who believe we do not grow or mature. Few besides my family even noticed."[3]
>
> – *Jack Trimpey*

The Rational Recovery® AVRT®5 system is based on recognising and defeating your Alcoholic/Addictive Voice. The idea is that you split off your addictive nature into a separate person, which they call 'the beast'. It's basically an externalisation of any internal problem, much in the same way as we discussed the 'god' problem or the idea of a demonic force inside (that say a Christian may term it). It's claimed in the book that this is a new and exciting idea, but as we know: it's not. You'll also know that this idea is touched on in the AA "big book" in the form of John Barleycorn, but anyway I digress. It's also not too dissimilar to the archetypal or symbolic figure that we as Satanists use.

By making your addiction another voice in your head that's not you, it allows you to take back some of your own control by recognising when your addictive voice is talking and how to say no to it. Becoming conscious of this addictive thought process was something I did in the very early stages of my recovery. I found that once the idea came into my head of drinking, I would play out how it would go in terms of a snowball effect.

This snowball effect would play out as follows:

I might get away with one drink now, but I would be letting myself down. I may be able to control my drinking for a while, but how long will that last: days, weeks, months? Did I want to go back to the way I was before I stopped drinking: look at how bad that was!

The snowball idea came from a ball of snow being rolled down a mountain. It starts off small, fitting in the palm of your hand, at the top but by the time it gets to the bottom it is the size of a boulder!

I later found out that this technique of essentially 'taking action by not taking action' is a process called Wu Wei, which is an important concept in Taoism.

This idea allows you to have thoughts about drinking or using and then saying the best course of action is, in fact, no action. By thinking about a problem, it doesn't mean that the problem is an issue in reality until you make it so. To think about drinking or using is not the same as drinking or using. The fact that you can be consciously aware of these thoughts is a huge step for most people with an addiction. Not acting on them is how the battle is won.

I feel like I should mention a few other recovery programmes that you can fully research yourself. The first of which is SMART[6] recovery which I think would be beneficial to those of you that get something out of the group discussion concept of the AA programme even if AA is not the correct fit. These are done online and led by members that have completed a SMART course. It isn't, however, a system that I'm all too familiar with although I do know a few people that have had successes through the programme.

I have also had some really great conversations with one AA member, who especially struggled with the 'god' concept of the 'AA way' for years, and had finally found peace in a sponsor who followed the Buddhist path. He was able to adapt the Refuge Recovery[7] concepts to fit his AA programme and gain the best recovery for him where he is now continuing on his longest stretch of clean time.

Refuge Recovery works on a mindfulness meditation concept and, from my conversations with people following that path, seems to have quite a few crossover ideas into the satanic philosophy that could resonate with some people, especially if it links in with some of the concepts of their own individual S-Theory.

One of the books from Refuge Recovery that was recommended to me was Dharma Punx: A Memoir by Noah Levine, although I've not had a chance to get myself a copy yet, I have to admit. Levine, though, was a punk back in his youth and would definitely appeal to those of you with a rebellious punk nature. He has written several books, and as Wikipedia states he "mixes his philosophical alignment with Buddhist beliefs and punk ideology" so if that sounds like you, I'd certainly be heading out to try that out.

There are also multiple left-hand path recovery groups on social media platforms that will be full of people trying all sorts of different ways to recover, some more successful than others, should you need any further guidance. A word of warning about social media groups, though, beware of those thinking their way is the only way possible or that if a programme didn't work for them, it can't work for anyone else!

[1] Dr Ed Day, Senior Clinical Lecturer in Addiction Psychiatry, King's College, London.

[2] Overview of treatment approaches – ugc.futurelearn.com. (n.d.). Retrieved from https://ugc.futurelearn.com/uploads/files/.../Overview_of_t reatment_approaches.pdf

[3] The Small Book: A Revolutionary Alternative for Overcoming Alcohol and Drug Dependence 3 (Rational Recovery Systems) by Jack Trimpey, Dell, 1995.

[4] Rational Recovery® Retrieved from http://www.rational.org/index.php?id=94

[5] Addictive Voice Recognition Technique (AVRT). (n.d.). Retrieved from http://www.rational.org/index.php?id=36

[6] UK SMART Recovery – Self-Management and Recovery Training https://www.smartrecovery.org.uk/

[7] Refuge Recovery – A Buddhist Path to Recovery from Addiction http://www.refugerecovery.org/

VIII

DISEASE VS CHOICE

Let's make this simple shall we: if you believe your addiction to be a disease or a choice, it shouldn't really matter that much if you are making a conscious decision do something about it. Even if you think addiction is a disease, there is no magic pill or potion to "cure" you of this said addiction, so other avenues need to be explored in dealing with this addiction issue. The 'Disease vs Choice' debate is still hotly contested amongst scientists in the field, with the majority of evidence leaning towards the disease side of the debate.

However, as I have stated before, if you find through your own research evidence to support whichever idea you feel is best, then you can add that to your recovery programme. You can always discuss why you have come to whatever conclusion you have settled on with those who are willing talk it through. I'd also like to point out that if new evidence is to come forth on the subject, then you are allowed to change your opinion on the matter.

IX

THE SCIENCE
OF ADDICTION

I would like to point out at the very beginning here that I am NOT a doctor, nor do I claim to be. However, I have done some extensive research for this section, but I am aware how fast the science of addiction moves and changes quite rapidly at times. I would, therefore, advise that you do your own research if you wish to question any of the points made in this chapter. All the information given below was factual to my knowledge at the time of going to print.

So let's start off by asking a question: what is addiction? Well as you may have gathered from the size of this chapter that is both a simple and a very complex question. I'm sure you will have a broad understanding of what addiction is about, but do let's pose this question that was used in my addiction study course at King's College London: "…would those of us who drink lots of coffee and get headaches if we miss our morning cup of coffee consider ourselves coffee addicts? Do we only think of the stereotypes of injecting drug users, the stereotypes of criminals or drug fiends?"[1]

Consider some of the words of Nora D. Volkow[2] from the US National Institute on Drug Abuse: Scientists began to study addictive behaviour in the 1930s. At that time, society deemed people addicted to drugs to be morally flawed, lacking in willpower or being completely selfish and it was these same views that shaped the responses to drug abuse. Society was treating it as a moral failing rather than a health problem, which led to an emphasis on punishment rather than prevention and treatment. Groundbreaking scientific discoveries about the brain and how it responds to alcohol and substance abuse have revolutionised the scientific world's understanding of addiction and helped advance a more effective response to the problem.[3]

Changing society's attitudes towards addictions has to be hard fought and very difficult to achieve. However, advancements in the scientific understanding of addiction have led to revolutions in the way countries and governments have gone about reducing these types of problems. One such book that documents this is 'Chasing the Scream' by Johann Hari[4], and I would highly recommend anyone wanting to make serious changes to their locally and nationally based recovery and addiction treatments to read this book.

A useful starting point on the science of addiction is to look at how a diagnosis of addiction is made; however, that is something that will be covered in more detail in the next chapter by C.M. Wulver[5]. I would also recommend his book that looks at Satanism and mental health called Satanic Health Mental Wealth[6].

Many recovery groups will talk about the inheritance factor of addiction, so that is something that we need to touch on, with genetic susceptibility accounting for maybe half of the risk for developing an addiction. Other risk factors will include those in the social and psychological environment such as the role of family and friends, parenting skills, peer pressure and socioeconomic status[7]. We'll discuss how these risk factors can increase the chances of developing addiction.

Addiction doesn't respect who, what or where you are, rich or poor or whatever[1]. Addiction happens, and it happens for a reason, it's functional and serves a purpose[1]. Alcohol and substance use can occur for a number of reasons: to remove our pain or sadness, help us cope with differing situations in life, or it just helps us relax and enjoy our spare time. Essentially what it does is it gives us something that we need[1]. The most obvious and fundamental initial experience is that drug use makes us feel good[1]; it relieves our worries and provides the escape that we are after. So yes, the initial decision to take drugs is typically voluntary one.

By voluntarily engaging in the use of alcohol or drugs, we are rewarded with feelings of pleasure and euphoria. We feel good, so we want to do it again. What drugs do and more importantly what drugs that are so often abused do so very well is that they overstimulate this rewards system. These drugs of abuse will increase a chemical within our brain called dopamine. Dopamine is a neurotransmitter. It is present in regions of the brain that regulate emotion, movement, cognition or thinking, the development of new memories, and most importantly, the feelings of pleasure. Therefore this is known as the dopamine reward pathway of the brain. This is the pathway that usually becomes activated when we do something that's important for our survival, like eating, having sex, spending time with our children, and so on.[1]

Some drugs can release from 2 to 10 times the amount of dopamine that natural rewards such as eating and sex do. In some cases, this can occur almost immediately with the effects lasting much longer than those produced by natural rewards. The resulting effects on the brain's pleasure circuit dwarf those produced by naturally rewarding behaviours. The effect of such a powerful reward strongly motivates people to take drugs again and again. This is why scientists will sometimes say that drug abuse is something we learn to do very, very well.[8]

The increased activity of the dopamine neurotransmitter in the reward centre of our brain is what gives us this great pleasure. Over time the brain will adapt to these overwhelming surges of dopamine. It does so by producing less dopamine or by reducing the functioning of the dopamine reward pathway to try to find a new healthy balance to the dopamine levels. This, of course, will impact not only the user's ability to enjoy the substances but also other aspects of their lives are significantly reduced because the impact on dopamine levels in the reward circuit of the brain can become so abnormally low that person's ability to experience any pleasure is greatly reduced.[7]

This is why a person who abuses drugs eventually feels flat, lifeless, and depressed, and is unable to enjoy things that were previously pleasurable. Now, the person needs to keep taking drugs again and again just to try and bring his or her dopamine function back up to normal, which of course only makes the problem worse, like a vicious cycle. Also, it will often mean the need to take larger amounts of the drug to produce the familiar dopamine high, an effect known as tolerance[8] that we will delve into a bit later in the chapter.

As we've seen drugs are chemicals that affect the brain by tapping into its communication system and interfering with the way neurons normally send, receive, and process information. Some drugs, such as marijuana and heroin, do so because they can activate neurons as their chemical structure mimics that of a natural neurotransmitter. This similarity in structure tricks the receptors and allows the drugs to attach onto and activate the neurons. Although these drugs mimic the brain's own chemicals, they don't activate neurons in the same way as a natural neurotransmitter which leads to abnormal messages being transmitted through the network. Other drugs, such as amphetamine or cocaine, can cause the neurons to release abnormally large amounts of natural neurotransmitters or prevent the normal recycling of these brain chemicals. This disruption produces a greatly amplified message, ultimately disrupting communication channels.[8]

The core structures of this reward pathway are located in what's known as the limbic system of the brain, which involves the prefrontal cortex, the very front of the frontal lobe, the nucleus accumbens, and the ventral tegmental area, the VTA[9]. Please feel free to look that up so you have a visual representation because it can be quite confusing. I also don't want to go too deep into an explanation of the structure of the brain as I am not an expert and the finer details are not relevant to the scope of this book. I encourage you to do your own research if the topic is something that interests you.

Over time and with frequent drug use the brain adapts to such a point that it's only in balance, meaning it is only functioning normally, whilst the drug is present in the brain[7]. When the drug starts to wear off or when we try to stop using it the brain becomes out of balance, and we experience an uncomfortable syndrome of signs and symptoms[7]. With continued use, however, an individual's ability to exert self-control can become seriously impaired, and it's this impairment in self-control that is a hallmark of addiction[10]. Brain imaging studies of people with addiction show physical changes in areas of the brain that are critical to judgment, decision-making, learning and memory, and also behaviour control[10]. Scientists believe that these changes alter the way the brain works and may help explain the compulsive and destructive behaviours of addiction[10].

There are two broad defining features of addictive behaviour that can be noted. Firstly, an increasing preoccupation with obtaining, using and recovering from the effects of a drug, so much so that other interests such as jobs, relationships are ignored. Secondly, continuing to engage in the behaviour to use these drugs despite being aware of the obvious physical, psychological or social harms and continuing to use despite attempts to stop.

Neglect of important areas of one's life to focus upon addiction inevitably leads to problems resulting in relationship breakdowns, jobs losses or health problems with these often the most debilitating aspects of an addiction[7]. Ironically, though, the stress caused can actually lead people to turn to further engagement in their addiction to relieve these symptoms and therefore become motivators strengthening addiction[7]. A vicious cycle starts to develop where addiction is characterised perhaps most dramatically by those people who continue to use drugs despite experiencing significant harms[7].

This concept of addiction as a compulsion and the inability to resist that impulsive need, that craving, marks many peoples' understanding of addiction[7]. It also, however, marks where neuroscience, pharmacology, psychology, medicine and addiction science are making the most advances[7]. We currently lack a single, unified theory of addiction[7]. But current research is taking us ever closer to such a theory, and within the last few years, some of the key neuroscientific and pharmacological components of addiction have been identified[7].

We know, for example, that the same sort of mechanisms involved in the development of tolerance can eventually lead to profound changes in neurons and brain circuits with the potential to severely compromise the long-term health of the brain[8]. For example, glutamate a neurotransmitter that influences the reward circuit and the ability to learn is altered by drug abuse from its optimal concentration[8]. The brain attempts to compensate for this change, which can cause impairment in cognitive function[8]. Similarly, long-term drug abuse can trigger adaptations in habit or non-conscious memory systems[8]. Conditioning is one example of this type of learning, in which cues in a person's daily routine or environment become associated with the drug experience and can trigger uncontrollable cravings whenever the person is exposed to these cues even if the drug itself is not available[8]. This learned "reflex" is extremely durable and can affect a person who once used drugs even after many years of abstinence.[8] This is another key aspect to understanding the systems to put in place to aid recovery for the long term.

To quote Dr Claire Troakes[11] in her video on brain function and addiction on my online course:

> "Several studies have shown that there is an increase in activity in the orbitofrontal cortex when drug addicts are exposed to drug- related stimuli. The nucleus accumbens projects to that orbitofrontal cortex via the thalamus and in turn the orbitofrontal cortex provides lots of connections back again to the nucleus accumbens. The orbitofrontal cortex also receives direct projections from dopamine cells in that ventral tegmental area, and it also receives input from other areas within the limbic system like the amygdala and the hippocampus[9]…
>
> Limbic regions like the amygdala, the septum, and the thalamus also provide input into the reward pathway concerning motivational and emotional factors. The reward pathway then interacts with the basal ganglia and the cerebellum to modify motor activity"[9]…

…which gives the science behind how and why these triggers for continued use can occur even without the drug being present.

One of the many things we need to look at is our tolerance to different substances and how this will affects us in our recovery. Tolerance occurs with the repeated administration of almost all drugs of abuse. However, the rate at which it develops to the drug's effects are not at the same rates or levels, and you can develop a tolerance rather quickly to one effect but slowly or not at all to another. Interestingly, tolerance often develops to the more unpleasant effects of the drug faster than the pleasant ones. For example, when you first start using a drug like heroin, which makes you feel nauseous and vomit, you'll find that you develop tolerance to that rather quickly, but you'll never develop tolerance to the constipation or the pinpoint pupils that are also produced.

The amount of alcohol or drug used increases as a response to tolerance over a period of time with the level of drugs that you're using or the amount of alcohol that is being consumed might reach levels that many would find astonishing. People using opiates such as heroin after a period of time can take doses and function normally at levels that might kill novice or first- time users. If a tolerance is developed to one type of drug, then a tolerance will also develop to all of the drugs in the same drug class. Meaning a tolerance to heroin will also produce a tolerance to the other opiates, such as morphine, codeine, and methadone. This is a phenomenon called cross-tolerance and can be very useful for the medical treatment of physical dependence with tolerance to a drug having important implications for understanding drug use and addictive behaviour.

Addiction will obviously cause people to spend more and more time seeking out the drug or the object of affection or addiction, using the drug and then recovering from its effects[7]. They will also continue to do this, seek, using and recover from a drug's effects, despite obvious harms to themselves and the people around them[7]. So although the initial decision to take drugs is voluntary for most people, the brain changes that occur over time affect self-control and ultimately the ability to see the future consequences of behaviour and the ability to resist impulses[7]. In other words, there is a compulsion to return the brain to that neutral balanced position of feeling 'normal', a process called homeostasis, which when referring to homeostasis occurring in the brain, is termed neuroadaptation.

Without tolerance reducing the amount of drug used and gradually stopping use altogether would be considerably easier and far more comfortable. Nevertheless, tolerance doesn't last forever, and it will drop down during periods of abstinence. Once we've developed tolerance to a drug and these effects start to wear off a range of uncomfortable symptoms may occur that could last from a few hours to a few days. These symptoms might include feelings of depression, aches and pains, nauseous or flu-like symptoms.

The uncomfortable signs and symptoms often experienced when drug effects start to wear off are generally known as physical withdrawal symptoms. Withdrawal symptoms represent the unopposed consequences of neuroadaptation, that balance and normality that was achieved after the regular presence of a drug becomes unbalanced and dysfunctional when the drug is no longer present. These are generally experienced as the opposite effects of the drug that was being used. For example, a drug that makes you feel euphoric or high then the withdrawal syndrome will be experienced as dysphoria (a profound state of unease or dissatisfaction), sadness or depression. Therefore as an addict, you will look for the things that will alleviate the symptoms as quickly as possible which inevitably mean by taking the drug you'll stop those symptoms immediately. In psychopharmacology terms, this process is referred to as drug tolerance and physical drug dependence. Withdrawal is an important concept, as for many, can also be a great motivator for continued use and why the need to find other ways to deal with these symptoms can be very useful in helping addicts stop and stay stopped in the long run. If our initial thought to any feelings of sadness or depression or general rebound symptoms is to reach for the learnt behaviour of drug use as the quickest method of elevating the symptoms, we need to find a way to rewrite this in the best way possible in our recovery process.

In the longer term, stopping the use of an addictive substance can leave us with a long- lasting feeling of sadness, dysphoria and cravings, which might last for months after we've stopped using a drug[7]. This is occurring because our brain is re-adapting to the absence of the drug and it's trying to get back into balance[7]. Tolerance and withdrawal put together, therefore, represent the biological components of addiction which some may call physical dependence or physical addiction[7].

An important factor affecting the severity of this physical withdrawal syndrome concerns the nature of the drug itself. Drugs vary in how long they take to clear them from the body. Some are metabolised fairly quickly, while others can take a long time before they are eliminated, and this is referred to as the drugs "half-life." The half-life of any given drug is how long it takes for the body to get rid of half of the dose. The intensity and severity of the withdrawal syndrome are inversely related to the half-life of a drug, meaning, the shorter the half-life, the more intense the withdrawal syndrome, but the shorter it will last. Whereas for drugs with a longer half-life, there will be a longer withdrawal syndrome, but they won't be as intense.

Although there is no panacea, one size fits all or quick fix to recovery, successful and effective treatments are available[7]. And research shows that combining medications with psychological therapy or counselling helps the majority of people[7]. Treatments that are tailored to an individual's circumstances and needs do even better[7]. But we need to remember that the journey out of addiction can be a very long one[7]. It's common for someone to relapse and start using the drug again[7], but it's also common for people to maintain abstinence once on the right programme of recovery for them. However, if you do relapse that doesn't need to be seen as a failure, but rather the need to learn about what went wrong and then try again, perhaps trying a different form of treatment[7]. This approach is what I hope you will find with this book: a way to use and combine the common recovery programmes available to you from your unique satanic mind frame. I hope it will allow you to tailor any recovery system to work in the best way for you as an individual.

[1] 1-04-What is addiction part 1 – ugc.futurelearn.com. (n.d.). Retrieved from https://ugc.futurelearn.com/uploads/files/ed/dd/eddd5fc3-6690-4409-a5c9-f929060e

[2] Nora D. Volkow, M.D., Director, National Institute on Drug Abuse (NIDA)

[3] Preface | National Institute on Drug Abuse (NIDA). (n.d.). Retrieved from https://www.drugabuse.gov/publications/drugs-brains- behavior-science-addiction/preface

[4] Johann Hari (2015). Chasing the Scream: The First and Last Days of the War on Drugs. Bloomsbury. ISBN 978- 1-620-408902.

[5] C.M. Wulver, UK Mental Health Professional

[6] Wulver, C.M. (n.d.). Satanic Health Mental Wealth. Retrieved from http://corsmerch.tictail.com/product/satanic-health-mental-wealth

[7] 1-05-What is addiction part 2 – FutureLearn. (n.d.). Retrieved from https://ugc.futurelearn.com/uploads/files/3e/09/3e0970eb- 0462-4e54-a649-701277b8

[8] Drugs and the Brain | National Institute on Drug Abuse (NIDA). (n.d.). Retrieved from https://www.drugabuse.gov/publications/drugs-brains-behavior-science-addiction/drugs-brain

[9] 1-08-Neuroanatomical basis of addiction. (n.d.). Retrieved from https://ugc.futurelearn.com/uploads/files/a7/76/a7762513- 9869-4643-8840-6f0db244

[10] Drug Abuse and Addiction | National Institute on Drug... (n.d.). Retrieved from https://www.drugabuse.gov/publications/drugs-brains- behavior-science-addiction/drug-abuse-addiction

[11] Dr Claire Troakes, Brain Bank Institute, Institute of Psychiatry, King's College, London.

X

DEPENDENCE OR ADDICTION?

The following words were written for me by C. M. Wulver, a UK based mental health professional, so that you may learn more about the technical diagnosis process within the context of this book:

> I have been asked to write a chapter on what we as Mental Health Nurses and consultants use to define what many people call an addiction.
>
> In the UK we use a clinical manual called The International Classification of Diseases (ICD-10), whereas our counterparts in the US use the DSM-5, both classify and code all diagnoses, symptoms and procedures.
>
> I hope after reading this many of you will recognise these issues as a dependence instead of addiction and support their path to recovery.

In 1964 the World Health Organization committee introduced the term "dependence" instead of the commonly used terms "addiction" and "habituation". The term dependence can be used in a whole range of drugs such as alcohol dependence or opioid dependence. The term can also be used with psychoactive drugs (drug dependence, chemical dependence and substance use dependence).

The International Classification of Diseases (ICD-10)[1] describes dependence in terms applicable across drug classes; there are differences in the characteristic dependence symptoms for different drugs.

The latest edition of the ICD-10 defines the dependence syndrome as being a cluster of physiological, behavioural and cognitive phenomena in which the use of a substance or a class of substances takes on a much higher priority for a given individual than other behaviours that once had greater value. A central descriptive characteristic of the dependence syndrome is the desire (often strong, sometimes overpowering) to take the psychoactive drugs (which may or not have been medically prescribed), alcohol, or tobacco. There may be evidence that return to substance use after a period of abstinence leads to a more rapid reappearance of other features of the syndrome than occurs with nondependent individuals.

Dependence refers to both physical and psychological elements. Psychological or psychic dependence refers to the experience of impaired control over drinking or drug use while physiological or physical dependence refers to tolerance and withdrawal symptoms.

The ICD-10 Diagnostic guidelines

A definite diagnosis of dependence should usually be made only if three or more of the following have been present together at some time during the previous year:

✴ A strong desire or sense of compulsion to take the substance;

✴ Difficulties in controlling substance-taking behaviour in terms of its onset, termination, or levels of use;

✴ A physiological withdrawal state when substance use has ceased or have been reduced, as evidenced by: the characteristic withdrawal syndrome for the substance; or use of the same (or closely related) substance with the intention of relieving or avoiding withdrawal symptoms;

✴ Evidence of tolerance, such that increased doses of the psychoactive substance are required in order to achieve effects originally produced by lower doses (clear examples of this are found in alcohol- and opiate-dependent individuals who may take daily doses sufficient to incapacitate or kill non- tolerant users);

✦ Progressive neglect of alternative pleasures or interests because of psychoactive substance use, increased amount of time necessary to obtain or take the substance or to recover from its effects;

✦ Persisting with substance use despite clear evidence of overtly harmful consequences, such as harm to the liver through excessive drinking, depressive mood states consequent to periods of heavy substance use, or drug-related impairment of cognitive functioning; efforts should be made to determine that the user was actually, or could be expected to be, aware of the nature and extent of the harm.

ICD-10 Diagnostic criteria for research

Three or more of the following manifestations should have occurred together for at least 1 month or, if persisting for periods of less than 1 month, should have occurred together repeatedly within a 12-month period:

✦ A strong desire or sense of compulsion to take the substance;

✦ Impaired capacity to control substance-taking behaviour in terms of its onset, termination, or levels of use, as evidenced by the substance being often taken in larger amounts or over a longer period than intended, or by a persistent desire or unsuccessful efforts to reduce or control substance use;

✱ A physiological withdrawal state when substance use is reduced or ceased, as evidenced by the characteristic withdrawal syndrome for the substance, or by use of the same (or closely related) substance with the intention of relieving or avoiding withdrawal symptoms;

✱ Evidence of tolerance to the effects of the substance, such that there is a need for significantly increased amounts of the substance to achieve intoxication or the desired effect, or a markedly diminished effect with continued use of the same amount of the substance;

✱ Preoccupation with substance use, as manifested by important alternative pleasures or interests being given up or reduced because of substance use; or a great deal of time being spent in activities necessary to obtain, take or recover from the effects of the substance;

✱ Persistent substance use despite clear evidence of harmful consequences as evidenced by continued use when the individual is actually aware, or may be expected to be aware, of the nature and extent of harm (WHO, 2016)[1].

Issues affecting alcohol consumption and alcohol-related harm

A variety of factors have been identified at the individual and the social level, which affect the levels and patterns of alcohol consumption and the scale of alcohol-related problems in populations.

Environmental factors include economic development, culture, availability of alcohol, and the comprehensiveness and levels of implementation and enforcement of alcohol policies. For a given level or pattern of drinking, vulnerabilities within a society are likely to have similar differential effects as those between societies. Although there is no single risk factor that is dominant, the more vulnerabilities a person has, the more likely the person is to develop alcohol-related problems as a result of alcohol consumption.

Here are some of the key findings from The World Health Organization:

Key facts

✶ Worldwide, 3.3 million deaths every year result from harmful use of alcohol; this represents 5.9 % of all deaths.

* The harmful use of alcohol is a causal factor in more than 200 disease and injury conditions.

* Overall 5.1 % of the global burden of disease and injury is attributable to alcohol, as measured in disability- adjusted life years (DALYs).

* Alcohol consumption causes death and disability relatively early in life. In the age group 20 – 39 years approximately 25 % of the total deaths are alcohol-attributable.

* There is a causal relationship between harmful use of alcohol and a range of mental and behavioural disorders, other noncommunicable conditions as well as injuries.

* The latest causal relationships have been established between harmful drinking and incidence of infectious diseases such as tuberculosis as well as the course of HIV/AIDS.

* Beyond health consequences, the harmful use of alcohol brings significant social and economic losses to individuals and society at large (WHO 2016)[2].

Carl Bard said a great quote that I feel anyone on their road to recovery should use. I have told my own brother (who is an alcoholic) to recite this when he feels he is tempted to drink. It goes like this: "Though no one can go back and make a brand new start, anyone can start from now and make a brand new ending."

I suffer myself from an illness called dissociative disorder, which is mentioned in my own book, "Satanic Health, Mental Wealth", and use this phrase when I feel at a low ebb.

[1] WHO | Dependence syndrome. (n.d.). Retrieved from http://www.who.int/substance_abuse/terminology/definiti on1/en/

[2] WHO | Alcohol. (n.d.). Retrieved from http://www.who.int/mediacentre/factsheets/fs349/en/

XI

Now a word from my sponsor...

I needed to talk about sponsorship as it's a major part of the 12 step programme, so I will be detailing how it works and why it's useful to both parties involved. However, at the end of my description, I thought it was only right to allow my own sponsor to write something on how he has found sponsoring me. He is my third sponsor of this nine-year period of sobriety, which began on 1st November 2007, but out of all of them, he has helped me progress the most and whom I've found the most connections with. It has been a more successful relationship because of our shared interests. There aren't many sponsors that will get excited at the idea of going to a Sunn o))) or Wardruna gig with you or tell you that maybe it's time to do some magick, not yet at least!

Sponsors are one of most powerful tools to help people stay sober in a 12 step programme. This individual is there to offer guidance and support to a sponsee. The sponsor is not only a person to guide the member through the AA programme but to also be there to listen. Being able to rely on a sympathetic ear can be particularly important when you are feeling on the verge of relapse. Choosing the right sponsor is important because otherwise, the relationship could prove to be disastrous.

There is both some good and some bad advice out there on how to pick a sponsor, but the general guidelines are that you pick someone of the same sex or sexual orientation as yourself. Make sure you choose someone who is sober and who has actually gone through the steps. You can't expect to get advice, or as some say mentoring, on how the 12 steps are done from someone who's never done it. You will need to pick someone who is secure and comfortable in their own sobriety; otherwise, their flakiness will rub off on you! By picking someone with long term sobriety will also mean that they will be able to spot the warning signs to a relapse and help to steer you away from it.

Some would suggest that you don't need to relate to the individual who is sponsoring you. Although I would say this factor is helpful, I would agree not overly important, as it's the system being used that should be your primary focus. I found I was drawn to those I related to because I liked what they said about how they used their system. My sponsor caught my attention when he mentioned being a pagan because he would rather worship Satan than a Christian god!

But you know you might not get it right first time round, but it's not like you've married the person: just get a new sponsor!

Your sponsor needs to be somebody who is completely trustworthy, as a lot of confidential information will get exchanged in this type of relationship[1]. An unscrupulous sponsor could try to benefit from this disclosure. Therefore, it is important to trust your instincts when choosing a sponsor as many people who go against this inner voice later regret it. Just because there are shitty sponsors out there, this does not mean, though, that every sponsor is just out to spread 'juicy' gossip on you.

It's also helpful to know if your sponsor has a sponsor, so when they are not sure of an answer, they have someone to go to. It will also keep him (or her) in check! Your sponsor will tell you truths about yourself that you don't necessarily want to hear, but this is vital for your own self-development and allows you to rid yourself of some of the deeply rooted self- deceit you may have. It's vital to get an outside perspective on situations especially if that person has also gone through something similar himself (or herself). They should also let you know when you've done something right as well, though! I'd say make sure you pick someone that has a sense of humour too as you could potentially be spending a fair bit of time with this person and the last thing you want is to add a dull, boring and lifeless person into the mix.

The best time to ask someone to be your sponsor is generally after a meeting, but there are no hard and fast rules on that as long as you ask someone! Just to clarify: you do only need one sponsor at a time to avoid getting conflicting advice. Remember everyone would have gone through the steps in a slightly different way and without knowing it, they would have tailored what was done to suit their own individual needs. This doesn't mean, however, that you can take conflicting advice from other people you talk to in the rooms either, though.

Most sponsors will tell you to contact them at any time, day or night if it is an emergency. The urge to relapse can come at any time, and having somebody to contact can make all the difference[1].

The focus in meetings is on members supporting each other, but many find they benefit from a one-to-one relationship with a sponsor more so. I found I opened up more on a one-to-one basis but found the group meetings were helpful, as well, in hearing other perspectives and gaining new insights as to how to overcome problems. It also gives you a platform to tell others how you've worked through a problem that may help them, which I think is even more important if it comes from a satanic perspective.

Sponsorship has been an important element of the 12 step programme since the beginning. The founding members realised that it was helping other people, which was keeping them sober. In fact, the organisation originated from one alcoholic reaching out to help another[1]. The idea of helping another go through the programme is much more selfish than you might think. What actually happens is, as a sponsor, you will be reminded of situations you would have dealt with previously and can see how far you've come.

Sponsorship can be hugely beneficial to both parties, but sometimes things do go wrong. The most common pitfalls to watch out for include some of the following things, so it's helpful to keep an eye out for them:

Some sponsors can be overbearing and will try to manage every aspect of your life[1]. They may be doing this out of a genuine desire to help, or it could have more to do a type of hunger for power[1]. Escaping addiction should be about finding your freedom, so allowing a sponsor to have too much influence over you is unwise[1]. You need to be in charge of your recovery. Your sponsor should just be there to advise. Sometimes the sponsor can be overly critical, and this can damage confidence and self- esteem.

If a sponsor relapses it can be devastating, and it may even put your own sobriety at risk. This is why it is recommended that members of AA always look for people with a strong foundation in recovery but of course, even then, there are no guarantees[1].

You'll usually provide your sponsor with a lot of personal information especially around Steps 4 and 5, and this can contain a lot of embarrassing information, as well as things that may even have legal implications.

Therefore, giving such information to an untrustworthy sponsor could later prove disastrous. If you feel that you like the way the sponsor works but don't feel happy about giving over all that personal information, don't. Go and see a professional to coincide with working with your sponsor, as confidentiality laws will bind that relationship.

You need to remember that sponsors are just people in recovery as well and they are just as liable to give bad advice, as anyone else. This is why it is crucial to not accept their opinion as infallible, and this is particularly important when it comes to medical advice[1]. There is no obligation to follow the advice offered by the sponsor[1].

Hopefully, that didn't put you off the idea of sponsorship. However, it's best to make you aware of where it can go wrong so you can avoid it. Obviously, though, when it works well it's great, and I leave this section now with some final words from my sponsor…

> "I am a recovered alcoholic and drug addict with, at the time of writing, just over 16 years of clean time and sobriety. Much of that time has been spent wrestling with the spiritual side of the 12 step programme and the conflicts that arise within the fellowship regarding the 'God' word.
>
> AA itself clearly states the following in one of its own pamphlets entitled 'The God Question':

'AA is not a religious organisation. Alcoholics Anonymous has only one requirement for membership and that is a desire to stop drinking. There is room in AA for people of all shades of belief and non-belief.'

The pamphlet goes on to say:

'Whatever you do, don't let someone else's religious beliefs prevent you from finding the solution that is available to you through Alcoholics Anonymous'.

This is often a difficult concept for many new converts or returnees to proselytising faiths to accept. In their fervour and zeal to spread their own particular brand of monotheism wherever they find themselves, their failure to accept the spiritual broad highway that is such a vital element of AA as a whole can be very damaging to those, like me, who have a completely different concept of a 'higher power' than the one to which they adhere. To this day my skin can start to crawl in a meeting when an alcoholic refers to 'the bigger book', a not so oblique reference to the Bible, or when another tells me that their recovery is courtesy of kneeling prayer to Jesus Christ and Jesus Christ alone, a figure that mysteriously provides the only 'genuine' portal to a supreme being who demands human sacrifice as a measure of faith and apparently allows his only son to be brutally murdered, in some way for my benefit.

I remind myself daily that I am fully entitled to my own definition of a higher power within AA.

Although some of the roots of AA and the 12 step programme itself do originate from a Christian based movement, a message carried from the Oxford Group by 'Ebby T' whose meeting with co-founder of the fellowship Bill W is recorded in the basic text of Alcoholics Anonymous, it is most emphatically not a Christian organisation, nor indeed is it associated with nor endorses any other faith, sect, or organisation. There really is only one requirement for membership and you are asked to consider and access a higher power of your own understanding, not anyone else's. This, I believe, is one of the main reasons that AA continues to flourish, whereas of course, all the Christian temperance movements have bitten the dust.

My own personal approach can best be described as an unholy mix of eclectic magickal belief and chaos magick. I believe that power in any 'God' is only invested in that 'God' through my own actions and faith. Once I have elected to take that action and invest that faith, this power becomes very real indeed. The proof is in my pudding — for this man to be writing this over 16 years since taking a drink or drug is a measure of that power.

It has been my privilege to work with Ben as his Sponsor in AA. Working with Ben has been a revelation and the time spent with him has benefited my own recovery greatly. This is, of course, what Sponsorship is all about. The benefits are as great for the Sponsor as they are for the Sponsee, especially when they are a good fit.

I jumped at the chance to work with a man who followed a spiritual path that was regarded as downright heretical by some in the fellowship. I knew exactly how he felt. In very early recovery a gentleman outside a meeting pointed at the rather small and innocuous pentacle earring I was wearing and told me in no uncertain terms that I needed to 'ditch all that stuff immediately' as it would, apparently, 'get me into all sorts of trouble' and lead to me drinking again. I dread to think what this chap thought of Ben walking into the same meeting a few years later in full black metal regalia complete with satanic slogans to the front and rear of his hoody. Over the years I have been shunned, mocked, laughed at and chastised in meetings when sharing about my own concept of a higher power and the actions that I have taken to access that power. Ploughing a lonely spiritual furrow in a fellowship can lead a man to doubt himself. Ben arrived at the perfect time on my own recovery to help me stay the course and I sincerely hope that I have been able to help him as much in return.

I was able to learn from Ben's practical action-based approach to the 12 step programme and as a result, up my own game. I was also gifted with introductions to alternative methods and styles of ceremonial magic, meditation and music, all of which remain an integral part of the maintenance of my own spiritual condition to this day. I doubt very much that I would have taken the time to read any of the works of Anton LaVey were it not for my relationship with Ben, nor would I have experienced extraordinary live performances and recordings from artists on the spiritual margins of the world of music.

The extraordinary amount of work that has gone into this book is also inspirational to those of us who are sometimes at risk of becoming the dreaded 'bar prop' he so wonderfully describes, a bar prop with or without a drink in hand. The 12 step programme is a programme of action, not a programme of thinking, and Ben is most emphatically a man of action − this is one of the main pillars of his own recovery and I am grateful to him for his hard work and commitment both to this book and to the 12 step programme itself."

[1] How to Choose an AA Sponsor − Alcohol Rehab. (n.d.). Retrieved from http://alcoholrehab.com/addiction- articles/how-to-choose-an-aa-sponsor/

STEP 1

WE ADMITTED WE WERE POWERLESS
OVER ALCOHOL – THAT OUR LIVES HAD
BECOME UNMANAGEABLE.[1]

This one is self-explanatory: if you don't admit you have a problem then you have nothing to fix!

The following are the 20 questions[2] that are proposed to see if you are an alcoholic, answer these questions as truthfully as you can.

1. **Do you lose time from work due to drinking?**
2. **Is drinking making your home life unhappy?**
3. **Do you drink because you are shy with other people?**
4. **Is your drinking affecting your reputation?**

5. Have you ever felt guilt or remorse after drinking?

6. Have you ever got into financial difficulties as a result of drinking?

7. Do you turn to lower companions and an inferior environment when drinking?

8. Does your drinking make you careless of your family's welfare?

9. Has your ambition decreased since drinking?

10. Do you crave a drink at a definite time?

11. Do you want a drink the next morning?

12. Does drinking cause you to have difficulty in sleeping?

13. Has your efficiency decreased since drinking?

14. Is drinking jeopardising your job or business?

15. Do you drink to escape from worries or trouble?

16. Do you drink alone?

17. Have you ever had a complete loss of memory as a result of drinking?

18. Has your physician ever treated you for drinking?

19. Do you drink to build up your self-confidence?

20. Have you ever been to a hospital or institution because of drinking?

How many questions did you answer yes to?

Alcoholics Anonymous say that if you answer three questions as yes then you have a problem. All mine were a yes!

Lots of people that are non-alcoholics always like to pick up on question 16. Do you drink alone? Because it's something that normal drinkers can do. Well, let me tell you there is a very big difference between having a few cans of beer on your own while watching the football, a movie or playing video games to the boxes of wine, crates of beer or bottles of whisky that I was putting away alone in my flat.

If you feel that you don't have a problem then, by all means, carry on the way you are and come back when you feel it's an issue. Unless you are willing to admit to yourself that something is a problem, when your own self- pride stops you, then you are not ready. No one should force you into a recovery process; in my opinion, you have to want to drag yourself back from the situation you have allowed yourself to create.

Once you admit that it is a problem, then it's time to take some action.

The point is you are powerless over that initial thought which invokes an emotional response based on a brain pathway to the reward sensation in the brain. What you need to do is become aware of the thought and block the pathway, and then reward the new action of not drinking or using.

In the words of Candice Shelby[3], Ph.D., Addicts are NOT Powerless:

> It is because of the unrecognised fact that everything we think about, every thought whatsoever, is as much emotional as it is intellectual, but our emotions operate largely unconsciously. The very way we learn the meanings of things — what things are, what makes up the world — is already emotional: for example, the first "object" of our knowledge, the mommy or caregiver, does not arise in the child as a purely intellectual concept. Babies develop the concept of this "object" by interacting with someone who soothes, comforts, and makes him feel safe and warm — GOOD — in addition to everything else that enables him to distinguish this person from all the other colours, shapes, movements, etc., entering and exiting his field of experience. In other words, people don't start by distinguishing objective things in the world, and only later decide on what kind of emotional "tags' they will have. Rather, the initial distinctions that we make among the entities that come to constitute our world are already full of meaning; things are comprehended in terms of their value or disvalue to us, and we perceive those values as attending their objects, whether consciously or not[4].

Addiction is our condition as humans—it's inherent in the way that we are built. The basic structures underlying addiction are the same structures that keep us seeking food, sex, and other things essential to life and the reproduction of our species is that addicts are not different from other human beings, except in some small but important details. In so far as we are all potential addicts in this more general sense, the very shape of our world is affected by the emotional value (or meaning) inherent in those substances which, at least in the beginning, make us feel so very GOOD[4].

Arguments and reasons have no power over emotion, which operates at a deeper level in our brains than does the higher reason of which we are so proud. That's why people can know more about recovery programs than anybody they've ever met, and yet be more susceptible to relapse than the simplest just entering into recovery. Once we understand the mostly unconscious operation of the emotional values connected with things in our lives, we understand how people's actions often move in precisely the opposite direction of what they know is good for them. Often, addicts know what is good for them, plan in good faith to do it, and then do exactly the opposite. Recognising the unconscious influence that emotion has in shaping their world, as well as in planning and executing their actions, can help addicts make sense out of ways of acting which would otherwise seem crazy, senseless, and/or uncontrollable[4].

All this may seem to argue for the opposite of my stated point: it may seem to show, that is, that addicts are, in fact, powerless over their addictions and that they should run as fast as they can to some higher power, to prevent them from doing further self-harm. But that is not the case. While it is true that addicts are unlikely to succeed in overcoming their addictions with no additional support, it remains true that the addict alone is the one who actually has power over his or her addiction.[4]

It is striking, but acceptance of just one fact, profoundly emotional in nature, can cause major changes in the meanings of things in a person's world. This fact suggests that once past the immediate stage of physical dependence, it is possible for addicts to change our emotional attitudes toward substances and activities that we know have nothing good to offer, and to change our lives altogether.[4]

Start to rewrite our emotional experiences and associations, which in turn has subtle effects on the way that we see the world.

Slips, real slips, do happen—and they are explicable in terms of our emotional grasp of objects and events in the world, and the connections of those emotional parts with the planning and acting parts of our brains. Slips are possible, that is because our attention is finite and our brains are very busy little bees, doing millions of actions per second. So, while we might "officially" think that we have a certain view toward a substance, our emotions may be operating in the background quite contrarily, moving us in a direction quite different from the one of which our conscious thought and judgment would approve. Being tired, stressed, hungry, or having had an interaction with someone that has left us hurt, disappointed, or angry, can distract us from our real goal, and can bring "online" emotional effects that drag us away from our true and helpful perception of the world, and back toward the one that did us such harm. For these reasons, mindfulness practice has great potential as a primary tool of sobriety whether undertaken as part of one's meditation or as a separate practice—and note that none of these practices implies any religious connection.[4]

In conclusion, it is not the case that addicts first have to admit powerlessness in order to become and remain sober. The unfortunate fact is that the power does not arise where or how we wish it would, that is to say immediately, and simply by thinking or deciding.[4]

If the addict can't change him or herself, no one can. The power is ours.[4]

I am powerless over my craving and my want. I want to use, but I am not going to. I am powerless over what I have been through in my past and how they make me feel, and by admitting that I am powerless through the first step I recognise that I can never again deal with things through my use. That's a fact.[4]

[1] The Twelve Steps of Alcoholics Anonymous. (n.d.). Retrieved from http:// www.aa.org/assets/en_US/smf- 121_en.pdf

[2] The Johns Hopkins Twenty Questions: Are You An Alcoholic? were originally conceived by, and need to be attributed to, Dr Robert Victor Seliger while he was a Department of Psychiatry faculty member at the Johns Hopkins Hospital in the 1930's. It was intended for use as a self-assessment questionnaire to determine the extent of one's alcohol use. It was not intended to be used by professionals as a screening tool to help them formulate a diagnosis of alcoholism in their patients.

[3] Candice Shelby, Ph.D., Associate Professor of Philosophy, Univ. of Colorado, Denver.

[4] Addicts are NOT Powerless – LifeRing. (n.d.). Retrieved from https://lifering. org/for-professionals-menu/addicts-are-not-powerless/

XII

ABSTINENCE INSTEAD OF COMPULSION

If you are truly going to embrace the philosophy of Satanism and become the best person you can be, then you need to look at areas in your life that hold you back or cause you problems.

As an addict or alcoholic, you need to embrace the concept of indulgence instead of abstinence but don't mistake compulsion for indulgence. Let's look at the dictionary definition of all three of these words shall we:

Indulgence:

[COUNT NOUN] A thing that is indulged in; a luxury: "Claire collects shoes—it is her indulgence."[1]

Compulsion:

1 [MASS NOUN] The action or state of forcing or being forced to do something; constraint: "the payment was made under compulsion."[1]

2 An irresistible urge to behave in a certain way: "he felt a compulsion to babble on about what had happened."[1]

Abstinence:

[MASS NOUN] The practice of restraining oneself from indulging in something, typically alcohol or sex: "I started drinking again after six years of abstinence"; abstinence from premarital intercourse[1]

If you feel compelled to do something, then you no longer have a choice over whether you do it or not. I felt compelled to drink, and once I started, I found that I couldn't stop. It was no longer something that I enjoyed doing: it had become toxic both internally and externally. I no longer wanted it, but I somehow needed it to perform basic functions in my everyday life.

How can you be the best person you can possibly be if you can't maintain appointments or you are stuck on the sofa hung-over; have cuts and scrapes on your face where you tripped and fell over when you were in blackout, or you got into a fight but can't remember how. How do you keep your job when you are late for work because you woke up on the wrong side of town after you passed out on public transport on the way home the night before. How do you explain why you are still wearing the same clothes you wore yesterday?

There came a point for me where I had to stop. I tried it out on my own without any structure or framework to build from. I'd get a few weeks in and see the positive changes that not drinking had made in my life; then celebrate with a drink and be back at square one again after only a few days of heavy drinking.

Having tested the abstinence theory and seeing the positive effects it had on my existence if only for a short time, I was able to stay away from my chosen poisons. My next task, my drive was to find a framework I could work from and a support network that I could go to when I needed advice.

With most aspects of my life, I knew the people I could go to that had the best knowledge to obtain what I wanted. For example, I knew who to ask for the best gear; I knew where to go to get a drink at 4am on a Monday morning; I knew who to ask for the best advice on the latest band to listen too, etc. But I had no idea where to go to meet someone that had recovered from a drinking problem. So my only option was to try the local AA meetings.

Another thing I feel that I need to add at this stage is that selfishness should not be confused with compulsion, either. Many people will confuse compulsion for a selfish act because the act will have a negative outcome. I would suggest that when people say they were selfish in their addiction (because they only thought of themselves) they, in fact, mean that their only goal was to get their addicted substance; this is not a selfish act but a compulsive one.

Let's look at the definition of selfish now:

Selfish:

[ADJECTIVE] (of a person, action, or motive) lacking consideration for other people; concerned chiefly with one's own personal profit or pleasure: "I joined them for selfish reasons."[1]

Whereas we have looked at the definition of compulsion previously, it being the action or state of forcing or being forced to do something or an irresistible urge to behave in a certain way, so the choice or control factor is removed from the equation. To be truly selfish we have to predetermine we are going to do something that is beneficial to us.

Too often the compulsion to drink or use becomes confused with selfish behaviour, in my opinion, and therefore is spoken about in a negative way. Let me ask you this question: is it a negative situation if I say no when I'm asked to put myself in a situation that might have me using again? I don't think so; is it selfish? Yes, of course, it is because I am only concerned with how the situation is going to affect me.

The point I'm trying to make is that you need to be completely selfish in your recovery and you need to start doing things for yourself and find what you are passionate about and do those. When you act on compulsion and do everything in your power to chase after the substance you are addicted to you are not being selfish.

So how do you know what's selfish and what's compulsive? Well, this can generally be defined by abnormal compulsive behaviour, which you may already be aware of but it will definitely come to the surface once you start looking at your behaviour patterns. To give you an idea of what abnormal compulsive behaviour is like, here are just a few examples from my own experience:

Many of my friends didn't really notice that I had much of an issue with my drinking; they just thought I was a lightweight until I actually spoke about some of the stuff they didn't see. I would generally need to have a few cans or bottles of beer before I'd go out and see my mates. I would also need to drink heavily when I got home and would often wake up in the morning holding on to a bottle of beer or bottle of wine.

Something I did a lot at the beginning in my mid teens was to snort aspirin because I thought it would thin the blood and get me drunk faster. I also did this because I didn't want to be a drug addict and I didn't want to do class A drugs. I also had to snort it because I couldn't take tablets; what's even more stupid is the fact that they were dissolvable and I could have quite easily dropped them in the beer I was drinking!

Little did I know that some years later I would be padded down by a drug dealer because of the amount of cocaine I wanted to buy off him on my second visit. I ended up taking a vast array of different drugs mixed in with my drinking by the end of my darkest days. I was fortunate that I never really liked them much; they just ended up being things that I'd do because I felt like it or the people I was with were doing it as well.

I ended up after one heavy night out taking LSD, which I was given by some random guy I met on a bus, right before a 3-mile walk home across Blackheath at 3am. I would do randomly crazy things like eating plants or looking for faeries under my mates' sofas while I was only drinking (and generally in blackouts).

[1] Stevenson, Angus. Oxford Dictionary of English. Oxford: Oxford UP, 2010. Print.

STEP 2

CAME TO BELIEVE THAT A POWER GREATER THAN OURSELVES COULD RESTORE US TO SANITY.[1]

The power greater than yourself at this stage is your 'godhead', your archetype, your symbol of yourself, Satan. The reason it cannot be you at this point is because you do not know enough about yourself, despite what you might think. The sanity you are looking for is breaking the cycle of drinking again and again and expecting different results from the disastrous ones you keep getting.

As you have just come to the conclusion that you have a problem with your drinking or other substance use, and have made a decision to do something about it yourself, you need to find a way to get that self-will back. Being a Satanist, you will be able to accept the responsibility for having done this to yourself. No one poured the drinks down your neck; no one shoved the coke up your nose or rammed the pills down your throat.

If you feel compelled to drink or use, then it has clearly become a programmed idea that you need the substance in question. You need to look at reprogramming your system. It's very difficult to reprogramme something that you cannot see or touch; therefore, we have to externalise this part of the self in order to remould it, fix the problems, add new components and get it running at an optimum level.

You don't try to fix your car engine with the bonnet down, do you? No, you need to open it up so you can take a good look at things and maybe even get the engine out for a more detailed look. You need to be able to use your archetype or 'godhead' to allow this to happen to yourself. You need to reconnect with that dark driving force of energy that lives within you. So if you are ready to do this, then you need to find out what you are looking at…are you ready to find yourself and stare into the eyes of Satan?

[1] The Twelve Steps of Alcoholics Anonymous. (n.d.). Retrieved from http://www.aa.org/assets/en_US/smf-121_en.pdf

XIII

ADDICTION HURDLES GOLD MEDALLIST

What I have noticed with myself in the few years before going to AA, in my early recovery and with other addicts/alcoholics in their own recovery, is they are forever putting hurdles and barriers in the way of moving forward or doing something. These are usually lame justifications or rationalisations that go along with those that will make the hurdle seem higher and more difficult to overcome. This behaviour is also a way for the individual to resist change and continue with a thought pattern of habits that has become comfortable.

Excuses like: I can't stop drinking because my only option is AA, I don't like or work well in group sessions, or I can't participate in the AA programme because of the focus on the God aspect. Then these people will seek out others, who will agree and confirm this opinion, to justify their decision not to change: "I don't drink as much as Noah, and he doesn't have a problem."

An excellent example of this was from someone I was speaking with on a group forum that had to partake in anger management sessions as part of his probation agreement. This individual complained publically about the sessions being a waste of time and commented: "in the last session we watched a Disney movie" so that other people would confirm to him that the sessions were a waste of time and that he didn't need to go through with them. I believe this individual was also seeking the confirmation, and excuse, so that they had someone else to blame if they were to fail: "it wasn't my fault; people in the forum convinced me the sessions wouldn't help".

So at this point, the individual expected people to agree with the opinion that the anger management sessions were a joke. Instead, I asked what movie they watched: "Inside Out" was the response. For those who haven't seen the film, it focuses on the internal emotional struggle of a girl and also shows her parents' internal emotional struggles. The film examines the connected emotions of Joy, Sadness, Fear, Anger and Disgust so you can see how this was entirely relevant to the treatment of anger management. (I'd also highly recommend the film!)

It was only after some probing that this individual was able to admit that viewing the film was, in fact, beneficial, but then came the next excuse! This entrenched behaviour was the norm for this individual; there was always an excuse or justification for why they were not able to change and why their current using was more beneficial. For example, this same individual had stated previously in the same forum that they had a drug test as part of their probation but had been using weed to combat anxiety issues and keep their anger in check. They asked the group what the best options were for this test; my advice was to admit to the drug taking and ask for help with the issues of anxiety and marijuana. A week later, this same individual came to the forum to boast about how they cheated their drug test and two weeks later again looking for congratulations on being two months off weed.

Let's just say I gave this individual a good dose of reality and showed him where the barriers were being put in place. The penny didn't drop during that conversation, and we are no longer in contact as I refuse to waste my time with people who are not willing to listen, but I hope I have planted a seed as to what his real issues are and I wish him the best with his recovery.

Once you get to the point where you can see these barriers in others, you will also start to notice them in yourself. I like to think about the meme, which pictures a horse tied to a light plastic garden chair with the quote: "Sometimes the thing that is holding you back … is all in your head." It's at this point that you will stop putting imaginary hurdles in your way and be able to combat the real ones with the vigour and determination for success that they fully require. It's here that you will become that Olympic gold medallist at the hurdles.

Obviously, you are not the only one to put obstacles in your way, and so problem-solving is an essential part of life. Finding a quick and easy method for problem-solving will help to eliminate problems before they happen. The simplest method I have found for this is 5 S's for success from the 9 satanic mnemonics.

The 5 S's are explained fully in Futureproof Adaptability[1] but here is a brief description of how they work. Kaizen (new spirit), as it was originally called on its creation in Japan, is designed to reduce waste and increase productivity on a whole. This methodical system comprises of five pillars, which are Sort, Set, Shine, Standardise and Sustain.

OK, so first of all, we are going to:

* **Sort** your problems into different groups;
* **Set** out a priority of importance;
* **Shine** or clear the area by making an action plan and following it through;
* **Standardise** this system for all your problem solving to increase your efficiency; and try to **Sustain** it.

Simple really when it's laid out like that!

[1] Banks, Lee. (n.d.). "Rational Satanism Futureproof Adaptability by CoRS Merchandising." CoRS, Web.<http://corsmerch.tictail.com/product/rational-satanism-futureproof-adaptability>.

XIV

8 SATANIC COGNITIVE REALMS OF EXISTENCE

I felt the need to add in this condensed version of the 8 Cognitive Realms of Existence[1] as I mention them quite often throughout the book and I didn't want you left scratching your head wondering what I'm on about! Remember, though, this is condensed; the full version can be found in the book Futureproof Adaptability[2]. I would suggest for you to fully understand the Rational Satanism philosophy and make your own subjective connections that resonate more with you, as an individual, rather than me telling you how I use and connect with it, that you delve further into the series yourself.

Right, let's get into it then! Satanism has no room for an external hierarchy, but an internal one ensures that we are crafting the right path to what we want to achieve[1] by crafting our own system and not mimicking someone else's. Satanism is about individuality, and the realms are individual to you, so walk them all[1]. No matter how long it takes, the Godhead will be reached, when all the personal blocks fall into place[1]. These set of tools are also an essential part of Paradigm Shifting which allows your recovery system to evolve and grow as you do. For each of the 8 Realms, I'm going to give you a brief explanation of what they are about. If, however, you'd like a more in-depth description of these I'd highly recommend the books in the Rational Satanism Collection[3].

1 **Revelation** – The initial revelation of turning to Satanism is considered a realm of its own, as for some it is a huge life changing step. It is also for this reason we named our Q and A gateway group on Facebook 'Revelation'. From this stage, the next step on the cognitive ladder is a simple step to make...

2 **Knowledge** – Knowledge and the quest for it is a large portion of what both the satanic community and the mind-set are about. The knowledge we absorb is what carves out our path and our direction of thought. So our next rung, of course, needs to be...

3 **Comprehension** – All of that knowledge you've acquired while searching in the second realm you'll need to make sense of. There is no point having a load of knowledge that makes no sense to you and furthermore can't be pragmatically applied. So for the next step, there has to be some form of...

4 **Analysis** – When you reach this personal realm the 90% 10% Thinking concept will truly come into play. You will be able to craft your own personal path and axiom of success, be it a logical or spiritual approach. It's while analysing and realising what you are and what works for you, that you will create your own personal thinking fraction and take you closer to the godhead. This is done by…

5 **Synthesis** – Essentially a complex whole formed by the process of combining. So now that you have acquired the knowledge, comprehended it and analysed the information you can easily create a combination of personal components to make your own personal system whole. It's here that you will have reached the final portion of dialectical reasoning and your path will now further itself on personal experience rather than knowledge. This is done by…

6 **Application** – When you reach this realm it's a level of experimentation and discovery. You have your ideas and personal understandings that you have resonated with in the other realms of practical applicability, and it's time to test them out. Once you have begun applying your system to your objective or subjective reality you can ascend to the realm of…

7 **Demi Godhead** – In this realm you are still taking on the self-personification, but you haven't ascended to the full godhead yet. While walking

this realm, you are still applying what you have learnt but are yet to fully know whether what you have created is going to get you personal success on every level. It's only when the realm of...

8   **Godhead** – is reached that you truly know the self and exactly what the self wants. You solidly have your personal fraction relating to your thought process and have attained the pragmatic maxim of applicability. This realm is yours and yours to own. It contains the large golden throne that the internal beast will sit in comfortably watching you reap the rewards that your system is bringing you.

As Satanists, we will always be on the quest for knowledge, but when the Godhead is achieved and understood, all the other realms become redundant, as all will take place in the Godhead realm. We understand ourselves to the extent that we have techniques in place that allow us to add to our personal system easily without having to wonder whether the "self" is right, we are now truly our own god.

[1] The Church of Rational Satanism – 8 Satanic Cognitive Realms. (n.d.). Retrieved from http://www.churchofrationalsatanism.com/essays/8- satanic-cognitive-realms/

[2] Banks, Lee. (n.d.). "Rational Satanism Futureproof Adaptability by CoRS Merchandising." CoRS, Web. <http://corsmerch.tictail.com/product/rational-satanism-futureproof-adaptability>.

[3] The Church of Rational Satanism – The Books. (n.d.). Retrieved from http://www.churchofrationalsatanism.com/the-books/

STEP 3

MADE A DECISION TO TURN OUR WILL
AND OUR LIVES OVER TO THE CARE OF GOD
AS WE UNDERSTOOD HIM.[1]

Don't get too hung up on that G-word. From a Satanic point of view – you are making a decision to take your life back from the compulsion that drove you to have a life that you feel is unmanageable or causing you a problem. Whether by design or accident and much to the chagrin of many a born again Christian in the fellowship, the AA 'Spiritual highway' is as broad as the people in it.

In this step we are starting to take our lives back and to do this, we need to start to understand how we see ourselves and how we want to be seen. To do this we need to use our 10% to create a symbolic figure that will represent us, our archetype, ultimately to create a Godhead or self-image for us to work towards.

So here is where you will need to do some of your own work; the following is the framework that I used at this point, but you are welcome to adapt it to suit the way you work.

Who is your symbolic figure?

The figure could be anything: Satan, Lucifer, Baphomet, Lilith, Odin, Thor, Freyja, Thoth, Mut – whatever you want. Don't just say I want to use Satan because he's cool. What do you know of the figure you have chosen? Why have you chosen them/it? Is it because they are most like you or because they are something you aspire to be like?

For the next set of questions, I find that mind maps work best for me, but you can use whatever method works best for you:

What characteristics does he/she/it have?
How do you relate to he/she/it?
What does Rational Satanism represent to you?

These questions are designed to give you a greater understanding of what it is you want from yourself, where you are and where you want to end up. Because you are able to essentially take 'you' to an external place, you can look at yourself from a new perspective. It allows you to stand back and see a bigger picture, remove the stuff you don't like, build on the stuff you do and add new parts that were not there to start with.

If at some point, however, you feel that you want to change your symbolic figure, then change it. You may find that you have either outgrown the previous one or you have found, after some more research, that it no longer represents who you are or what you want to be. If you do decide to change it then just go through this process again so that you have a clear understanding and grounding of who or what that is.

WARNING: do not start thinking of yourself as some all powerful being, because YOU ARE NOT! You are still a human being and cannot control other people.

What you aim to obtain is the power to take charge of your own destiny and become the master of your own reality.

Once you have sorted out the areas of your archetype that you would like to aspire to, you need to devise a plan of action. We will also be looking at plans of action in the following steps where it might also be beneficial to rework your archetype to better suit your needs.

There are several ways in which to do this, either start with the point at which you are at now and work forwards, or start from the end point back to where you currently reside. You will need to create smaller goals that work towards the end goal in order to see a continuous chain of events.

Granted if your archetype has wings, you will not physically grow them! However, if you research the meaning of the symbolism of wings, it is suggested that they are an ancient symbol of divine power and therefore could represent your ascendance to your godhead through the 8 Cognitive Realms of Existence.

If, however, you dream of flying, then you should devise a plan to take flying lessons to become a pilot, book a tandem hand glide flight, take a trip in a helicopter, skydive or bungy jump. Only you are able to put limits on yourself, and you need to take responsibility for your recovery and where you want it to go. Following these steps will not be like taking a magic pill. If you are not willing to take the responsibility to plan how you are going to achieve the things you set out to achieve, you will not achieve them.

I would suggest that you, therefore, think about each aspect that you attach to your archetype. Meditation is a good tool for this. However, don't spend weeks or months on this idea in an attempt to "get it perfect". Your archetype is not set in stone and will evolve and change as you grow and learn new things about yourself through your recovery and your study, where you will take on aspects of your archetype and then add new ones to achieve.

> "The room for self-improvement is the one that you never finish decorating"
>
> – *Lee Banks*

[1] The Twelve Steps of Alcoholics Anonymous. (n.d.). Retrieved from http://www.aa.org/assets/en_US/smf- 121_en.pdf

XV

ARCHETYPE

My original archetype was Oden (spelt with an e, it is a derivation of the old Norse, Óðinn). I liked the fact that he hung himself from the world tree for nine days to receive the knowledge of the gods. I also liked the idea he had a set of gods, both good and bad, at his disposal.

One of the things that it was suggested for me to do, at the beginning of my recovery process, was to pray. There was no way I was going to get on my knees for anyone. So I found an Odenist prayer that I used to say to myself into the mirror in the bathroom before I went to work.

This is the one I used:

Hail Mighty Asa-Thor!

I go forth today to do my duty.

I go forth today to drink deep life in Midgarth.

Walk beside me, great friend of man.

Lend me your strength, that I may defeat
all Jotuns in my path,

Be they giants of the world, of the mind
or of the heart.

Help me do right by my kin, as you do.

Hail Thor!

I found that the passage repeated in the morning gave me something to focus on in the early part of my day. I also got myself a set of runes that I would come to use every day and still do now. I found that, after a while, I was saying the phrase less and less and just focusing on the rune of the day.

The rune, I know in my rational mind, has no influence on me in any way unless I choose it to, of course. I like to think of the meaning behind the daily rune as something that I either need to be aware of or look out for in the day.

I had looked to join an Odenist group and met with a member who was also in AA, but found that it wasn't for me. It was around this time that I felt that maybe

Oden wasn't the right Archetype for me and maybe I should look to change it. I thought long and hard and did quite a bit of research on who and why, as in Step 3. I chose Satan. I went down a more satanic path than I had done before.

I brought back the idea of saying something in the mornings as a way to connect with my new archetype; it was from the Satanic Scriptures[1]:

Hail Satan full of might!
Our allegiance is with thee!

Cursed are they, the God adorers,
and cursed are the worshippers of the
Nazarene Eunuch!

Unholy Satan, bringer of enlightenment,
Lend us thy power,

Now and throughout the hours of our lives!
Shemhamforash!

I no longer feel the need to say this in the morning, before I leave the house or on the way to work. Initially, it's a great tool, but it is simply a learning aid that should be removed like the stabilisers on a child's bike, once you're able to continue without the additional support.

I kept the runes going throughout the whole process, and it's the only thing I do on a daily basis now. Although I must admit some days, I do forget. If I'm able to, I'll do it there and then when I remember, or

I'll just wait until I can do it, even if it's the following day. I mean the world isn't going to end just because I've not read a rune. Also not having done it, is not going to send me into such a spin that I'm going to start drinking again. Something only has that kind of power over me these days if I allow it to.

XVI

BIFROST TO RATIONAL SATANIC LIVING

"A bridge to normal living" is a term that gets used quite often in AA meetings to explain what the programme gives you. Of course, there are issues with that statement, and yes you can pick it to pieces; for example, what is normal living, etc.

Do I believe that if I don't attend regular AA meetings that I will drink again? No. My normality wasn't sitting in draughty church halls every night of the week; I was still fortunate to hold a job and have a family, so I needed to also share my time with them.

Granted my life was at a point where I needed to change it, but if it was a choice between sitting in an AA meeting and "having fun" drinking, I know what many people would choose.

For me, the rooms are just another tool in my recovery toolbox. I use meetings to hear others' ideas and processes for how they overcome problems in their own recovery journeys and see how I can adapt things to work for me in my personal recovery.

When I first attended AA, I went to two to three meetings a week; many people recommended that I did 90 meetings in 90 days and I can see how this would be helpful for those who don't work or live alone. Support is needed at this early stage, especially as I have been told medical journals state that it takes a full 90 days for the central nervous system to stabilise after drinking.

I had spent two years trying to combat my drinking issues on my own. So I felt comfortable enough to be able to handle two or three days "on my own" before I would start to find an excuse to drink. At which point I would go to a meeting for support, to listen to what the group said and if I didn't want to share with the group, speak to people individually before or after the meeting. Personally, I will only share stuff with the group if it directly relates to what the main speaker has said.

My meeting habits are now quite sporadic, as I only go when I feel I want or need to go. It's that idea of support again: If I need it, I know it's there. But I need to work on things on my own, to some extent, as it's my path to recovery, and I don't want to be left clinging to the rooms for the rest of my life.

I find that as long as I do things that I feel are right for me and discuss those with an outside source (like a sponsor) from time to time, then the necessary support is maintained. The benefit you get from an outside perspective on the matter, the ability to see a full picture, inject some new ideas and a different view on things is extremely valuable to maintain your recovery.

I wouldn't recommend long periods away from meetings, especially in the early days, as they help you to deal with issues that will constantly be new to you. Meetings will give you that support network because, just like first learning to skate, you will need to hold on for support more often.

Once you feel you have a footing for how to deal with problems, then why not see what happens. As long as you are self-aware enough to know when to reach out for support, or seek advice/help, before reaching for your substance of choice, then you will have a greater independence when your system or programme is in place.

If you are attending an AA meeting for the first time expecting everyone in the room to be free from drink and drugs, or having multiple years of sobriety, you will be in for a shock! As I'm sure you will be told: "the only requirement is the desire to stop drinking". Everyone is on his or her own journey (well some people are doing other people's journeys, but we'll get to that later!). And much like life, everyone is at a different stage of the journey and with varying levels of success.

When attending an AA meeting, I would suggest you listen out for the problems you can relate to, so you can hear how that person dealt with the problem and try to implement that into your system or programme of recovery. Remember you DO NOT need to share in a group environment if you do not want to. I find that if I relate to people, then I will seek them out after the meeting to have a conversation on a one-to-one basis. If I find I can logically see how the other person overcame a problem I relate to, then I will decide if I think it is a rational option for me to try.

I will only share in a meeting if I feel like I have something to say. Remember if you have something to say, you are probably not the only one that has that opinion and there may be others desperate to say the same as you.

Acronyms and stupid phrases really piss me off in AA, and it's one thing I try to avoid repeating. However, I'm not going to begrudge people using them if they find them helpful, after all, we are all on our own recovery journey. Sometimes I find I might say them to myself, like the popular HALT (Hungry, Angry, Lonely, Tired).

I will usually laugh when I do it, but it makes me aware and conscious of my behaviour. If I'm getting ratty or angry for no particular reason, it just reminds me that it might be an idea to message a mate to go for a chat over coffee, go and get something to eat or get some rest. Anger as an emotion will turn into a great passionate rage if we let it. And this typically forces us to make irrational decisions that can lead to drinking or using, so I find it's best to cut things off early, so as not to cause any problems. I'd also like to point out that this does not mean that I never get angry because believe me, I do!

Eating for me is still a very easy thing to forget to do, even with my length of non-drinking. I also know that I can get quite cranky when I don't eat, which can add to my anger and irritability issues.

Tiredness is also a big factor in my irritability levels. So if by thinking HALT to myself, I sit down and have a cup of tea with a biscuit, have a chat with a friend, a general chat with someone about a random subject or a power nap: it can stop me from that irrational thought process that could lead me to a drink.

I would also go as far as to say that my approach is the rational option, as opposed to not doing it because I don't like acronyms! That would be considered counterproductive pride and not helpful in any way.

Obviously, one of the biggest bugbears is the term Good Orderly Direction that is used by some atheistic members to replace the word 'god'. Personally, I don't think it's needed, and if you have read the two chapters on God, you will understand why I never needed or liked that phrase.

"Take what you like and leave the rest": that makes perfect sense to me. It was something I was told early on in my recovery, and it fits exactly with the rational satanic way of thinking. It allowed me to take the steps and the process to formulate my own journey and leave the Christianity out as I didn't find it helpful.

---

[1] Where does the 90 days come from? (n.d.) Retrieved from http://www.e-aa. org/forum/viewtopic.php?f=36&t=9840

STEP 4

This is where you look at yourself; probe to find out who you are and what makes you tick.

At this step, we are going to take a deep and detailed look at ourselves. Through the process laid out over the next few pages, we want to discover the attitudes, thoughts, beliefs, fears, actions, behaviours and behaviour patterns that are blocking our paths. We want to uncover the truth about ourselves.

This step is the main one: the one that's gonna kick up all the shit and remould you. I'm not going to lie; you are going to unearth things that are going to leave a bitter taste in your mouth. You are going to have to deal with things that you have buried away for a long time to help you move forward. You are going to find out that on some occasions when you thought you were right you were, in fact, the one in the wrong. The truth can be painful to hear, but it's the only way of learning and moving forward.

NOTE: It is advisable to have someone go through this process with you, to make sure you don't miss behaviour patterns because you still have a deep-rooted attachment to a situation. It is also advisable that this person is someone unconnected to you; this stops them having any attachments to things that may come up and hidden motives.

At this point, some people like to write a life story to get it all out. If you feel that that's what you want to do, then go for it. Try to be as detailed and as thorough as you can but remember you can always go back and do it again at a later date if you feel you need to. I'd suggest that it is done in pen and paper too, not typed on a PC or laptop. Some of the notes and mistakes you make along the way can be very enlightening when you look back on them. It also makes deleting a bit less easy!

For me, I found the idea of writing a life story too absolute, and I was forever trying to wedge stuff in three weeks later that I'd forgotten. I wanted a way that was more fluid and fit with my scatty brain but was visually okay to look at. Personally, I'm a bit of a neat freak when it comes to things like this, and I like things to have an order so that they are quick and easy to find when I need to reference back to them at a later date. Typically, I will scribble stuff down and then tidy it up after if I feel I need to.

I found that mind maps worked best for me, so I started with key events in life: childhood, home life, school, work, relationships, drinking situations. When I found that I had a key point that I could work stuff out from, I'd make that into a new mind map starting with that point. After a while, you will find that you create a web and a multi-layered representation of your life.

An example of one of my mind maps and a very simple question that can be extremely hard to answer at first for me was: 'reasons why I drank'. To give you an idea of the things that came up for me on this question I have put them in a list below:

* To relax
* As a celebration
* As a commiseration
* Boredom
* I thought it's what I needed to have a good time
* To be social: "it's what everyone else does"
* Confidence
* To change the way I felt
* To enjoy myself
* To numb my emotions

- ✱ To talk to women
- ✱ To overcome my shyness
- ✱ To let off steam
- ✱ To get a 'buzz'
- ✱ To overcome fear
- ✱ To mask my true feelings
- ✱ To overcome feelings of shame and low self- worth
- ✱ Because I was happy

As you can see, quite a few things came up for me: both positive and negative. Let me tell you, though, that at the end: none of my drinking was very positive for me!

One of the points I'm sure that will stick out is: 'I thought that's what I needed to have a good time'. Well let me tell you, you don't. If you believe that the only way to have a good time is to be off your face, then there is something clearly irrational going on in your head. In my dark days, I thought the sign of a good night was when you had to be told about it the next day because I'd blacked out and forgotten what happened. By going through this process, I was able to come to terms with the fact that I didn't actually like me and so I did everything I could to not be alone with myself.

Like with the previous step, do it as well as you can for now because you can always go back and add to it at a later date. Just because the steps have numbers doesn't mean that you can't go back to them in a different order at a later date or if you feel it would be beneficial you can do them all again if you have had another paradigm shift. You might find that having understood something from this process that you need to go back to change your archetype as well and that is fine too.

[1] The Twelve Steps of Alcoholics Anonymous. (n.d.). Retrieved from http://www.aa.org/assets/en_US/smf- 121_en.pdf

XVII

WRATH OF CAIN!

"Being able to understand that some choices I've made have been based on older issues is all well and good, but it doesn't stop me wanting to punch Dave from accounts in the face because he's a twat!"

It is helpful to look at the past, but it's the here and now where we can make the most change. Yes, I'm sure Dave from accounts probably is a twat, but the fact you didn't get along with your dad is not going to be the reason for that! Have you ever thought, though, that you might partially be to blame for why he's a twat to you? Do you lash out at things when you are frightened? Do you act out and unwillingly hurt people you care for with a venomous tongue? Does your partner not wanting to be intimate with you last night cause you to have a bad day?

Maybe a tweak in your attitude can stop a few of these things and free up valuable brain space to do things you enjoy, rather than constantly run over situations in your head or deal with the consequences of acting on one of the areas of concern below.

This is where you need to work on day-to-day issues that we can have a direct effect on. To do this, we are going to look into four areas:

* **People we have harmed**
* **Sexual conduct**
* **Fears**
* **Resentments**

Add people, places and things to these lists as and when you need to, hourly if necessary! I found, with a lot of this process, the 'AA guidelines' wedge the God aspect in when it is not needed. So I have removed the Christian element for you so that it is not something that causes you to have difficulty with the process, as the process is very rewarding.

Here is a set of four worksheets that you can use to help you with this process. Some things will show up that you may feel are viewed as a negative, that aren't. The tables are designed only to make you aware of what you do and why you do it. It is left to the individual, using their own opinion, to decide what a positive or negative outcome is in these lists. For me being selfish is not a negative thing, and that may be the case for you unless it causes you issues.

FEARS

What am I afraid of?	Why do I have the fear?	Which part of the self have I been relying on which has failed me?	What part of the self does the fear affect?	What is my action plan to tackle and overcome my fear?		
List the people, places and things or anything else you fear.	Why am I afraid?	Self-Reliance		What are you going to do to face or remove your fear?		
		Selef-Confidence				
		Self-Discipline				
		Self-Will				
		Self-Pride				
			Self-Esteem			
			Pride			
			Emotional Security			
			Finances			
			Ambitions			
			Personal Relations			
			Sex Relations			

HARMS

Who did I harm?	What did I do, or fail to do?	What part of the self caused harm?	How was I at fault?	What should I have done instead?		
List the people, places and things that you are angry with:	Why am I angry?			What should I have done to achieve a better outcome?		
		Self-Will				
		Self-Esteem/Ego				
		Emotional Security				
		Material Security				
		Pride/Defiance/Independence				
		Self-Pity				
		Self-Reliance				
		Personal Relationships				
		Social Ambitions				
		Sexual Ambitions				
		Financial Ambitions				
			Selfish			
			Self-Seeking			
			Dishonest			
			Inconsiderate			
			Frightened/Full of Fear			
			Lack of Self-Discipline/Self-Control			
			Playing God–Trying to Control Others			
			Self-Centred/Ego-Centric			

RESENTMENTS

I'm resentful at:	The cause:	What part of the self was hurt or threatened?							Where was I to blame?					
List the people, places and things that you are angry with:	Why am I angry?	Self-Esteem	Pride	Emotional Security	Finances	Ambitions	Personal Relations	Sex Relations	Selfish	Self-Seeking	Dishonest	Inconsiderate	Frightened/Full of Fear	Try to be more specific as to where you may have been at fault

SEX CONDUCT

Who was it?	What did we do?	Where was I at fault?	What did I arouse?	Who did I harm?	What should I have done?		
List the people, you have experienced sexual conduct with:	Ask yourself what you did:	Was I Selfish?		Who was harmed?	Try to think about how you could have handled the situation better to achieve a more desirable outcome:		
		Was I Dishonest?					
		Was I Inconsiderate?					
		Was I Self-Seeking?					
		Was This Relatiosnhip Selfish?					
			Jealousy?				
			Bitterness?				
			Suspicion?				

132

Now is probably a good time to remind you of the Nine Satanic Sins[1] as laid out by The Church of Satan:

1. **Stupidity**
2. **Pretentiousness**
3. **Solipsism**
4. **Self-deceit**
5. **Herd Conformity**
6. **Lack of Perspective**
7. **Forgetfulness of Past Orthodoxies**
8. **Counterproductive Pride**
9. **Lack of Aesthetics**

It is worth keeping these in mind when you go through the everyday process of looking at yourself. Hopefully, after a short while, you will no longer need to use the pen and paper method of the tables to see the results, as you will be able to clearly see how a situation has manifested and know the steps required to get the results you are after.

I think, as well, while we are on the subject of Wrath it might be an idea to talk about anger and anger management, as I can still be prone to bouts of rage myself. Anger management does not mean internalising or suppressing anger ; it is a perfectly normal human emotion and, when dealt with appropriately, can even be considered a healthy emotion[2]. Of course, you are going to feel angry especially when we are dealing with sensitive subjects that relate to our own self-image. These feelings of anger can lead us to say or do things that we later regret[2]. Anger can also reduce our inhibitions and make us act irrationally[2].

The management of anger focuses on recognising the triggers for the emotion as early as possible and expressing these feelings and frustrations in a cool, calm and collected way[2]. This is one of the things that the worksheets are designed to help you with.

You will often have learnt-behaviours as to how you deal with strong emotions, so anger management is about unlearning ineffective coping mechanisms by learning more positive ways to deal with the problems and frustrations associated with anger you feel[2].

There are loads of anger management techniques that you can learn and practise, so if the ones I've laid out here don't work for you, then have a look at some other methods. However, if this doesn't help and you experience a lot of regular anger or rage, then seeking professional help will be much more effective.

It is important to recognise when you feel angry or experience feelings that may lead to anger[2]. You shouldn't try to suppress your anger but instead try to understand it and act in a positive way to alleviate negative aspects of your anger.[2] A preferred method of mine is the 'one man mosh pit' usually involving full volume blasts of 'God Hates Us All' by Slayer, 'Kill' by Cannibal Corpse or 'Hatred For Mankind' by Dragged Into Sunlight while I headbang my way to happiness!!

The hormones that we release when we are angry, which are mainly cortisol and adrenaline, are similar to those produced when we are stressed. The release of these hormones is an evolutionary trait, biologically produced to help us to escape from danger.[2]

When you exercise regularly, however, your body learns how to regulate your adrenaline and cortisol levels more effectively. People who are physically fit have more optimum levels of endorphins and it these endorphins, hormones that make you feel good, that are likely to make you feel less angry.[2]

If you are worried about having a conversation that may leave you feeling angry then try to take control of the situation[2]. Write down a set of notes beforehand, planning what you want to say in a calm and assertive way, this way you are less likely to get side-tracked during your conversation, especially if you can refer to your notes[2]. It can be helpful to identify what made you angry in the first place[2]. If possible explain to the other person what made you angry, but only if it is safe for you to do so, and by that I mean you are sure the other person won't just use the information to get a rise out of you. However, it is more important to focus on a way to resolve problems so that they don't arise again in the future[2]. Don't be afraid to stop conversations and to walk away from them when you feel you can deal with them at a better time later to suit you. I have on quite a few occasions told my wife, point blank, that we need to stop a conversation; that

I need to have five minutes alone before I get angry and to prevent a breakdown in resolving the situation.

Don't go into a full on rage at someone; they are less likely to listen to what you have to say and more likely to rage back. Wait until you have calmed down and then express yourself in a calm and collected way[2]. You need to be assertive without being aggressive[2] but if you do manage to misjudge the situation: taking responsibility and apologising for your actions can move the resolution in the right direction faster than you think. I'm not telling you to apologise to everyone either; some people need to be told what a dickhead they are!

Of course, you will need to accept that everybody is different and that we cannot control the feelings, beliefs or behaviours of others[2]. Try to be realistic and accept that people are the way they are, not how you want them to be[2]. If you don't like someone's opinion, which can happen a lot in AA meetings, just try to avoid or ignore that person as your time is better spent making yourself better as opposed to getting annoyed that they are not doing or saying things that you agree with. Being resentful or holding a grudge will only increase your anger and make it more difficult to control[2]. Avoid conversations that may make you angry especially when you are feeling tired, distracted or stressed as this will hasten your quickness to anger. I call this the Jenga effect: it's where you let little things stack up on top while, at the same time, destabilising the foundations by letting some of the smaller things build up; it will only be a matter of time before everything comes crashing down over a somewhat insignificant matter.

It is easy to use inappropriate sarcasm when angry but it's better to try to resist the temptation to do this and instead work on introducing some good humour into potentially difficult conversations[2]. This can, however, be a very difficult thing to judge, especially if you and the other person don't share the same sense of humour or it's a very delicate subject. Therefore, you will need to assess the situation for yourself to decide what is appropriate. If you can, however, introduce some humour then resentment will be reduced, and your mood lifted, and the simple act of laughing can go a long way to reduce anger, especially over the longer term[2] and can often be a good bonding tool.

[1] LaVey, Anton S. (n.d.). The Nine Satanic Sins. Retrieved from http://www.churchofsatan.com/nine- satanic-sins.php

[2] Anger Management – Self-Management Techniques. (n.d.). Retrieved from https://www.skillsyouneed.com/ps/angermanagement.html

XVIII

NUTRITION
AND EXERCISE

In the groundbreaking guide to the myths and realities of alcoholism[1], James R. Milam, Ph.D., and Katerine Ketcham highlighted the importance of diet to a recovering alcoholic:

> **Malnutrition.**
>
> All alcoholics are malnourished to some extent because excessive alcohol intake interferes with the body's ability to absorb and use various nutrients regardless of what the alcoholic may be eating. The cells, of course, are dependent on an adequate supply of nutrients to perform their everyday function, heal themselves, and create new cells.[1]
>
> Alcohol's massive assault on the structure and functioning of the alcoholic's cells cannot be reversed just by removing alcohol

from the body — abstinence alone does not make malnourished cells healthy again. The cells need vitamins, minerals, amino acids, proteins, fats, and carbohydrates, and they need them in therapeutic amounts and proportions. Without an adequate supply of these nutrients, the cells cannot get on with the long process of repairing the damage done by excessive drinking.[1]

Most recovering alcoholics do not even know that they are suffering from nutritional damage, and even if informed about the condition, they probably do not realise that a balanced diet and nutritional supplements will help them make a rapid and complete recovery. As discussed above, they are more likely to suppose that their psychological distress is caused by psychological problems — a misconception widely shared by society and by most therapists as well.[1]

Hypoglycaemia

When the blood sugar drops to abnormally low levels, the alcoholic experiences symptoms of fatigue, headache, sleepiness, forgetfulness, inability to concentrate, moodiness, anxiety, depression, hunger and shakiness. Alcohol immediately brings the blood sugar level up and makes the symptoms disappear. After one or two drinks, the hypoglycaemic feels remarkably better. His headaches and sleepiness are gone, and the mental confusion, depression and anxiety miraculously fade away.[1]

Hypoglycaemia is a chronic condition. The symptoms do not simply disappear when the alcoholic stops drinking, and he must therefore carefully regulate his sugar intake to control the level of glucose in his blood. This can be accomplished through simple dietary measures.[1]

A good suggestion that was made to me when I first came into recovery was the 'Mars Bar' trick. When you feel that you are getting a craving for alcohol, it's a good idea to have a Mars bar. I would keep a pack of the mini ones in the cupboard. The idea is that the body is not actually craving a drink but the sugar that it got from the alcohol and so you can kill off the craving by eating something sweet. I must say that I found it worked well for me.

One thing I can still struggle with, although I do eat healthily, is remembering to eat regular meals. I work on my own and can get so engrossed in what I'm doing that food can be the last thing on my mind. I can also be standing in front of a full fridge and not see anything to eat because during the day I just want to grab stuff to eat so I can get back to what I was doing before.

> The only way around this is forward planning: by either making a meal at the start of the day or reheating a meal (that usually my wife has prepared for dinner the night before). I also have a set of snacks that I can just pick up when I stop for a coffee or tea break during the day. Additionally, I found that factoring in eating to my time management plan drawn up at the beginning of the day was also a good habit to adopt.

During my research, I also looked into how our diets can aid our recovery: from areas where they might show us where a problem may lay to how altering our diet might take the edge off of cravings.

I came across a wide-ranging article by Deanne Alban on the Be Brain Fit website which discussed the importance of 'balancing your neurotransmitters to take control of your life' and I share some of her insights below:

> Neurotransmitters, as we have previously found out, are chemical messengers used by the brain cells to communicate with each other[2]. They exert a great deal of control over many aspects of life[2]. By recognising the symptoms of deficiencies in the most influential neurotransmitters, you can take appropriate steps to bring your brain chemicals and your life back in balance.

Serotonin

Low serotonin level symptoms include binge eating; insomnia, anxiety, negativity, digestive disorders, low self-esteem, low libido and hyper vigilance. Men and women also differ in their suffering with women have mood disorders and carbohydrate cravings and men being impulsive, having ADHD-like symptoms and excessive alcohol consumptions.[2]

People with low serotonin and addiction issues will tend to gravitate towards opiates and alcohol to self-medicate low mood and depression. Regulating serotonin levels may help take the edge off mental pain driving addictions, painkillers and heroin.[3]

To increase serotonin we need to look at the amino acid precursor or building block of serotonin called Tryptophan, it's found mainly in protein-rich foods like meat, eggs, fish and dairy. The relationship between serotonin, tryptophan and food, however, is not that straight forward. Both serotonin and tryptophan levels drop after eating protein-rich meals as protein blocks the synthesis of tryptophan into serotonin, and so a carbohydrate heavy meal or snack will allow for tryptophan to enter your brain and boost serotonin levels.

That being said your best options for a serotonin boost according to research are daily exercise, sufficient sleep and exposure to sunshine.[2]

Dopamine

This is released when your needs are about to be met and delivers a feeling of satisfaction when you've accomplished your goals[4]. The amino acid Tyrosine is a major building block of dopamine synthesis and can be found in most animal food products; however, other foods that increase dopamine include avocado, green leafy vegetables, apples, beetroots, chocolate, oatmeal, nuts and seeds. You can also include on that list two of the most popular hot beverages on the planet, coffee and green tea, so you don't need to turn into one of those boring twig and berry eating, water only drinking, health food nutcases, unless you want to, of course!

People with low dopamine levels and addiction issues will tend to gravitate towards dopamine mimicking drugs like cocaine and methamphetamine. Regulating dopamine levels with natural remedies may help take the edge off addictions in general and specifically addictions to those hedonistic highs previously mentioned.

Physical exercise and meditation increase dopamine levels but small things like accomplishing a goal or taking on new challenges also help to raise dopamine levels.

Therefore, breaking down long-range plans into short-term goals will help you get the dopamine boost and give you the motivation to continue. Every time you tick something off your 'to do' list you get a little high due to the dopamine boost.

GABA

Gamma-aminobutyric acid is a relaxing neuro-transmitter dubbed 'nature's Valium'. This brain chemical normally puts the breaks on an as-needed basis, but when you're low in GABA your mind gets stuck in the 'on' position.[2]

Typical symptoms of low GABA are being easily stressed out, overstimulated and overwhelmed. You may also experience lying awake with racing thoughts, feeling dread for no particular reason, experiencing heart palpitations, cold hands and shortness of breath.[2]

Low GABA is associated with anxiety disorders and panic attacks as well as physical disorders such as irritable bowel syndrome[2]. People with low GABA and addiction issues will tend to gravitate towards tranquilisers and possibly the mellow varieties of cannabis and downers to self-medicate low anxiety.

Regulating GABA levels may help to take the edge off these types of addictions.

Adding foods such as bananas, broccoli, brown rice, citrus fruits, fish, lentils, nuts, oats, organ meats (such as liver and kidney), spinach, and whole grains are among the best foods for increasing GABA[5]. All kinds of exercise can increase GABA, but yoga, in particular, stands out. One study is said to have found that just a single one-hour session of yoga increased levels by up to 27%[6].

So there we have a great list of foods that can be added to our diets to help us gain a natural balance and when put together with the right therapy can help to transform your life. The combined lists of foods above are as follows:

* Meat
* Eggs
* Fish
* Dairy
* Avocado
* Green leafy vegetables
* Apples
* Beetroot
* Chocolate
* Oatmeal

* Nuts
* Seeds
* Bananas
* Brown rice
* Citrus fruit
* Lentils
* Organ meats (such as liver and kidney)
* Oats
* Spinach
* Whole grains

Now for me, at the beginning of my recovery, that list would have got my head in a right mess, despite having spent time working for a pizza delivery company and working as a 'chef' in a pub. So I thought I'd give you some recipe ideas, which you can easily look up, to throw into your everyday diet.

Chocolate oatmeal beetroot cake; fish curry with spinach and brown rice; hardboiled egg with avocado and chicken sandwich made with whole grain bread; steak and kidney pie with carrots cabbage and mash; liver and bacon with brown rice and a creamy mushroom sauce; fruit salad; tomato and lentil soup.

Things like nuts and seeds can be ground and added to sauces. Achieving a positive change may be as simple as switching to whole grain bread from a white loaf and adding some nuts to your breakfast cereal. Nuts also make for a good snack as they are small and easy to carry.

When it comes to exercise in recovery, you will need to tailor a programme that fits your own needs and based on what it is you enjoy doing. Exercise is a great way to increase your dopamine levels which will help to take the edge off during your recovery. I have found doing a weights circuit at home, some fitness DVDs, Freeletics (body weight training), Black yoga (covered in the later chapter – Prayer, Ritual and Meditation) and 5-a-side football have all been great additions to my health in overcoming addiction. Exercise will also give you something to help break up the day, especially helpful if you are not in full-time employment. It will help give you goals to work towards, something else I found useful. Accomplishing goals, crossing off tasks and establishing a streak, or run of days, where you stick to doing a task for a set time will also increase dopamine levels. However, above all of that, it will help to externally show your internal transformation, which sometimes can be hard to see, not just for others but also for yourself.

At the start of my recovery, I was quite lucky that the job I was doing was a physical job, so exercise wasn't something I lacked, walking on average 7-8 miles a day. A demanding job can also have its downside as it meant I would be quite physically tired at the end of the day. As a result, I'm fit, but never achieved the muscular physique I would have liked because I find bulking up difficult, as even to maintain my current weight I need to consume 3500 calories a day.

I may not have reached my physical ideal, but having said that, let's not forget a fundamental part of human existence: the ability to have fun and laugh, not just with others but also at ourselves.

It is known that laughter has beneficial effects on our bodies. These effects are the result of activities in different regions of the brain that are triggered by humorous stimuli and by laughter itself. Studies have shown that brain regions normally involved in emotion, cognition, vision and movement all respond to laughter. For example, the midbrain and hypothalamus – the regions where dopamine is released in response to pleasure stimuli – are activated by laughter. Dopamine is the major component of the 'reward' pathways: it reinforces pleasure-seeking behaviour and influences our happiness.[7]

In addition to its effects on dopamine release, laughter stimulates the release of other feel- good substances, including endorphins, which are opiates capable of relieving pain and growth hormones, which play a role in growth and metabolism. These substances, among others released in response to laughter, have broad physiological effects, such as decreasing blood pressure and bolstering immune function. Many people agree that laughter protects one's sanity too, which is probably related to its ability to release stress and ease tension.[7]

How many recovery programmes tell you to have fun? I mean the reason we took these substances, to begin with, was because we enjoyed how they made us feel and they were fun. If we can attach behaviour that will benefit us in the long run to happy memories, then this will encourage us to do it again. You need to look at what you enjoy doing and things you are passionate about, other than taking the substances that got you to this point in the first place, obviously. Simple things like being creative and listening to music are also great ways to increase dopamine levels as well as potentially therapeutic in their own right, so draw some pictures, pick up those headphones and pump out your favourite tunes.

[1] Milam, J. R., & Ketcham, K. (1988). Under the influence: a guide to the myths and realities of alcoholism. Toronto: Bantam Books.

[2] Balance Your Neurotransmitters to Take Control of Your Life. (n.d.). Retrieved from https://bebrainfit.com/balance-neurotransmitters/

[3] Balancing Brain Chemistry with Peter Smith. (n.d.). Retrieved from http://www.balancingbrainchemistry.co.uk/peter- smith/70/Addiction-with-Natural-Remedies/Drug-Addiction-With-Natural-Remedies.html

[4] Schultz, W. (2001, August). Reward signalling by dopamine neurons. Retrieved from https://www.ncbi.nlm.nih.gov/pubmed/11488395

[5] Braverman, E. R. (2013). Younger brain, sharper mind: a 6-step plan for preserving and improving memory and attention.. Emmaus: Rodale.

[6] Deans, E. (2013, March 15). Yoga (ba) GABA. Retrieved from https://www.psychologytoday.com/blog/evolutionary- psychiatry/201303/yoga-ba-gaba

[7] Funny Science: Why Do We Laugh, and Can It Really Help … (n.d.). Retrieved from http://blogs.britannica.com/2008/07/funny-science-why- do-we-laugh-and-can-it- really-help-healing/

XIX

Money, Budgets and Time Management

This I think is an area that gets overlooked quite a lot in the recovery process, but it can be the cause of many significant worries and stresses in recovery. Sadly though when many people think of budgeting, they see it as depriving themselves of things, and so it's avoided much in the same way a diet would be . However, much in the same way as a diet is just a program for eating; budgeting is just a program for spending. In fact, just like a diet, which is just a word used to describe what you eat, a budget just describes how you spend. You will actually have a budget in place now even if you are unaware of it; it's just that it's unbalanced, overflowing and depleted in the wrong areas.

If you are hitting a mental roadblock when you hear the word budget then just call it something else, like 'personal financial planning', 'money balancing' or 'spending management'. That's all budgeting is, taking a proactive approach, rather than a reactive approach, to managing your money. It's not difficult to implement or just for people with limited funds; it can be an essential tool for achieving your life goals by planning in advance and prioritising where your money goes. For many of us just by having a solid budget in place, knowing how much money we have and exactly where it is going makes it easier for them to sleep at night.

Both my mum and my step-dad were accountants, and so from the age of 12 I had a bank account with a monthly allowance instead of pocket money; I was encouraged to keep a record of my monthly spending in the same way they did so that I would develop some financial capability. I would also like to add that, despite this, I still managed to end up in financial difficulties in my late teens. At this point, my parents even monitored my account for a time to try to regulate my spending, which only seemed to make matters worse during my addiction and it did take me a few years to rectify these issues. I'm not going to lie to you: my wife does the household budget now, but I still manage my own personal accounts. We each have a set percentage of our salary that goes into covering the house budget, and we discuss what goes where each month so we both know where the money is being spent.

There are quite a few systems you could use to track your money, and they can be as simple or complicated as you want, or as low or high-tech as you like. Just pick something you find easy to work with; it could be something as simple as a notepad and pen or an uncomplicated spreadsheet. For a more sophisticated solution, you could use financial software like Quicken and Microsoft Money or even an online app.

Once you've decided on your chosen system, you will need to keep track of every expense, especially the small ones as these will build up quickly. Make sure you update your budget daily by trying to allocate a time to do it at the end of every day. It's also really helpful to plan your budgets by calendar month and not by the dates you are paid; this will hopefully ensure an even flow of spending rather than a purge and starve scenario. You will need to make allowances for fixed and variable expenses. I know, for example, I've been caught out a few times by the odd expense that hasn't been included in my monthly plan. Most of all though make sure, where you can, to plan for occasional expenses to treat yourself.

This is all easy of course if you have a regular income. However, if you're paid hourly, on commission, are self-employed, work seasonally or are a student, you probably won't know how much you're going to make until the end of the month. Irregular pay makes budgeting a little trickier, but it's still feasible, so don't use it as an excuse. You will still need to cover certain expenses no matter what, and if you've been in the same line of work for awhile, you probably have a good idea of the minimum amount of money you're likely to make, so it's advisable to plan things around the minimum figure. Yes, I understand that this can be very hard; I was at one point having to work 30 hours a month overtime on top of my 37 hour week, just to break even on my outgoings that I felt were already stripped back to their lowest.

All you have to do is change the income and spending categories to reflect your personal situation. Then copy the sheet 11 times, so you have a worksheet for each month of the year. This makes it easy to plan in advance as well as look back on past months and see how you did. Most importantly you need to allow yourself to be flexible. If, for example, you want to spend more on groceries one month because you plan to have some friends for dinner, there's nothing wrong with that, but you will need to compensate in other areas to keep the balance. Don't expect to always stick within the amounts that you set for yourself as guidelines when you first created your budget; you will need to adjust and evolve your guidelines as you track how your spending is going.

As I touched on earlier, make sure to leave room in your budget for some fun things. Maybe your budget is so tight that the most fun you can afford is to buy the ingredients to make some chocolate chip cookies, but at least allow yourself that. For most of us, our lifestyle tends to inflate when income does, and there is nothing wrong with that. If you reward yourself the same way when you are on a six figure salary to that on minimum wage, where's the incentive to work harder? If you don't reward yourself, it will be emotionally difficult to stick to your budget in the long run.

Always make sure though that you keep your spending below your income. I know many of us tend to give off the impression that we are on a higher salary than we actually are so you need to be careful. Special events like birthdays will also need fit into your budget, and that's why it's important to have the year planned out if possible, rather than trying to pile the gift purchases onto a credit card to worry about at a later date.

Don't go into debt for things that are not long- term investments like loans, when you finance a car, for example, not only does it depreciate every year, cost money to maintain and eventually become obsolete, you're also losing money on interest every month. Long-term investments like a house or an educational course that you can reasonably afford should try to be built into long-term goals, especially if that course could get you a higher paid position at work resulting in an increase in wages.

Budget planning can also overlap into the time management aspect that I will get to in a minute. So if you plan errands so that you don't make multiple trips, for example, plan the food shopping on the way home from work on a Thursday night meaning you'll have the weekend to spend with the kids or doing things you enjoy. Maybe try to go to places that will allow you do more than one, it might not contain our favourite shop for food, but we sometimes go to the retail park where we can get a few different things at once saving you time and fuel if you're driving. If you have the space, bulk buying is also a great idea or stockpiling non-perishable foods when they are on sale, as long you remember to clean out the cupboards every other month by incorporating these foods into your meal plans.

This is only a brief overview on budgeting, largely based on Budgeting Basics[1] by Amy Fontinelle, but the more detailed version is available online.[2]

Another area that I found had a big impact on my life was my time management; I was very good at procrastinating, and that left me open to times of boredom which usually let my mind wander, and thoughts of drinking would creep in. The procrastination was also making me less productive in areas of my life that I needed actually to be doing things, like work projects; these would then add to my stress levels which would send me in the wrong direction to the old coping method of drinking, I was so used to.

I found this time management technique[3] especially effective.

Firstly you have to categorise your time into three distinct categories:

* **Thoughts**
* **Conversations**
* **Actions**

It's then suggested that you record your thoughts, conversations and actions in terms of brackets of time over the course of a week, so you can see on average how much you spend on each of these. If you find that you are spending too much time thinking or conversing about a problem rather than taking action to solve it, then I would suggest the 5 S's to Success from the 8 Cognitive Realms of Existence, which can help speed up the process and increase the action portion.

I found spending 20/30 minutes at the start of my day, while having a tea or coffee, to plan the day ahead was really helpful. It's also good to allocate blocks of time for things that you feel can take over your day. I can find that my researching needs to have a cut off time or I can read up on different things for countless hours. It's also helpful to block out unproductive distractions like social media and give them particular time slots during the day or only use them on your "breaks". I also found that lists of jobs that needed doing were helpful to show how productive I was being in a day by counting how many had been completed, as well as helping me remember things I needed to do. Prioritising jobs is also a good thing to get into the habit of doing; I also try to get a few small things ticked off a list before a break too as a psychological boost. I know it's quite lame, but I actually add things to the bottom of my lists just so I can cross them off; it's good for that dopamine buzz too!

[1] Fontinelle ,A. Budgeting Basics – Documents. (n.d.). Retrieved from http://documents.tips/documents/budgeting- basics-570a33ad6b955.html

[2] Budgeting Basics – Setting Up A Budget | Investopedia. (n.d.). Retrieved from http://www.investopedia.com/university/budgeting/basics 2.asp

[3] Joe Mathews, Don Debolt and Deb Percival. (2011, May 01). How to Manage Time With 10 Tips That Work. Retrieved from https://www.entrepreneur.com/article/219553

STEP 5

ADMITTED TO GOD, TO OURSELVES,
AND TO ANOTHER HUMAN BEING THE
EXACT NATURE OF OUR WRONGS.[1]

If you can admit to yourself and more importantly your 'godhead' where you have been at fault, you are taking responsibility for your actions. By sharing these details with another person that may have had previous experience of the same issues, it helps you to deal with them and move forward.

Essentially this step is where you look in more detail at what you have just done in the previous step. You have to be willing to take responsibility for the actions you took that were destructive or had a negative outcome. If you can admit where you may have been at fault in a situation that had a negative outcome for you, then you are able to learn from it.

Admitting where you were at fault to yourself can be hard, but it is even harder to admit it to someone else. Doing this makes you more consciously aware of your wrongdoing and will have a greater impact, as you will gain another's perspective on the situation. This allows you to get a viewpoint that you may not have considered if you have been too focused on one minor detail.

From the everyday process of looking at yourself in the present, using the four worksheets from Step 4, and examining the past with the mind maps or life story, you should be able to see clear patterns of behaviour that are both constructive and destructive. We are then put in the position of making a choice. Do I continue with my behaviour in spite of my knowledge? Or do I accept my behaviour has been destructive and make the necessary changes?

This choice is pure power and control and the exact opposite of powerlessness. Granted, at this stage, we will need help and guidance from others who have experience dealing with these same issues. This process again places us in a position of using power to do what is needed to make changes to the behaviours that no longer work for us.

Our thoughts create our emotions, and these thoughts and emotions can trigger the body's "fight or flight" response. This thought was created by you, created out of data in your brain from an external source without any relevance to what is real at that moment.

This thought process is how we generally operate: reacting to external data and acting on it as though it is a universal truth. The fact is we build our life around beliefs we have formed which may often be based on faulty data. This data is likely to be flawed because it only comes from our own subjective viewpoint, which is naturally biased to satisfy our personal needs and ego. By gaining another person's perception of the data, one that has not been distorted by the overall situation will hopefully be able to give us, as we strip away the self and the ego, the help to look at it from the 3rd side.

If you would feel more comfortable going through this process with someone qualified in this area like a therapist then, by all means, do that. I think many people feel worried about opening up to someone, especially someone without professional expertise because of either the fear of bad advice or the thought that confidential information will be used against you at a later date. For me, this has not been the experience, and I have both seen a therapist and gone through things with a few sponsors along the way.

That is also another point; you do not have to keep the same sponsor throughout your recovery process. You will find, through paradigm shifting while undertaking the activities in the Step 4 worksheets, that you may not agree with some of the suggestions or the way of working that your current sponsor has, in which case just get a new one: that is fine. However, don't use it as an excuse to constantly change and never actually do any of the work involved.

I found that both options were worthwhile: the professional therapist would make me question myself more, but the laid back, friendly, practical advice from my sponsor has helped me no end because I can see how it works in the real world and not just from a leather couch under scientific conditions. I also think the process was worthwhile for my sponsor too, as it made him look again at his own recovery and we would both bounce ideas off each other. It does help that my sponsor was a fellow chaos magician though and we don't need to go into too much unnecessary depth to understand each other's viewpoints.

[1] The Twelve Steps of Alcoholics Anonymous. (n.d.). Retrieved from http://www.aa.org/assets/en_US/smf-121_en.pdf

Step 6

Were entirely ready to have God remove all these defects of character.[1]

Take your 'defects of character' and move them into your 'godhead'. I like to think of them more as aspects of my character that I wasn't able to use properly. Calling them defects of character is like someone who has never been taught how to drive complaining that the car is faulty because they keep stalling it! In the 'godhead', these no longer become issues in daily life: these defects now become tools for you to use as and when required.

OK for this aspect, you may have to humour me for a bit as I take you through my thought process to get to the stage where I can pass on the final idea. However, I thought by showing the process I went through, it would allow you to pick up the chain at any point and be of more help to you. Below you will see the basic flow of my thoughts, and I will go through each of these in more detail shortly.

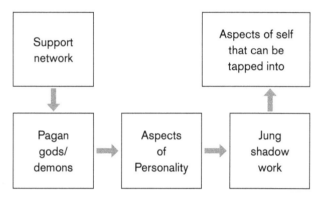

SUPPORT NETWORK

For me, this involved a few different groups: my family, my friends and also the people within AA. At times I've had to keep some of them at a distance while I've dealt with things, especially family so that I could avoid hurting them. Friends, or more precisely people I thought were friends, who were just after a free ride, or psychic vampires have been removed from my life. My true friends have remained very close and have been a great asset to my recovery.

A great example of this was at a music festival about two to three years into my recovery. My wife had left a pint of cider next to her bag while she went to the toilet. I noticed the bag was about to be kicked, knocking over her drink, so I picked up the pint to avoid spillage. To my surprise, three of my friends almost jumped on me; one of them nearly snatched the pint out of my hand. They were all very concerned and asked what I was doing. When I explained, we all laughed, as they feared I was going to drink it. Having seen the change in me over the last few years, they didn't want to see me go back there.

For that, I would truly like thank them for being there for me, whenever I have needed them over the years, and where I can, I try to do the same for them.

For the AA perspective, in the beginning, I'm very glad that I had a place to go. It was somewhere I felt comfortable talking about how I felt, about not drinking, with people who were in the same position or who had gone through it. Yes, I heard some shit in meetings, but then again I listened to some shit in the pubs I used to drink in.

I wasn't afraid to offend people by saying how I felt, because it was how I felt, and that wasn't going to change. I knew others could relate to it as well because they would tell me, and we would talk about how they did things, and they suggested ways that might help. In the UK we have a sizeable contingency of atheists in AA, and so I was able to swerve a lot of the 'god squad' meetings.

I don't feel I need the meetings very much at all now, but I still go when I can, and I'll tell you why. I keep going to AA meetings because somewhere out there is someone in the same position I was in and they need to hear there is another way to recover than relying on this Christian God shit! (or to put it more politely: there is another way to recover than being forced by others to rely on their obsessive fixation of the Christian God dogma!) It always makes me spit venom because I am living proof of this and the fact it works without 'god'.

Another reason I found the rooms of AA to be worthwhile is that it removed me from the comfort of my confirmation bias. It made me question things I may not have done, it angered me to the point of reaffirming my belief and understanding in things, and it gave me time to contemplate on processes.

PAGAN GODS/ DEMONS

I had a good understanding of the pagan gods before attending AA, so they were one of the first concepts I considered when the thought of a 'Higher Power' was suggested. I liked the fact that there was more than one; that they were not always good; they would manifest into humans and animals (a physical thing you could see and touch). I found thinking in terms of demons was quite useful as well at times, but this can be whatever works for you really as none of them are real.

I liked the fact that they all had different personalities and were almost like real people. I'm a very visual person, so I had no trouble imagining them all sitting round a table and allowing me to go to them when I needed them.

The visual aspect I had was a similar set-up to how a lot of AA meeting are set up. One of the suggestions for people having trouble with 'god' in AA was to "let the rooms be your higher power at the beginning". I found after a short while, though, that I started linking the personality traits of the gods to my support network: my friends, family and members of AA (good and bad).

ASPECTS OF PERSONALITY

Because I was able to humanise the pagan god concept, I took this one step further and started to look at the idea we spoke about in the 'God Problem'. What if these different gods and demons are all different representations of my subconscious? Were they different aspects of my personality? Had I unknowingly externalised it in order to deal with it in smaller pieces? (I came to find out later that this was how I use my 90% 10% Thinking to remarkable effect, although at the time I wasn't aware it was called that).

Well if I had, that piece of the puzzle seemed to fit, then why was I using an aspect of someone else's ego? I needed to make these into my own Gods and Demons so that I could use that to represent me completely. So I looked into the best way to do this which flows very nicely into the next section.

JUNG SHADOW WORK

I'm only going to give you the basics here and not go into extreme detail how to do this. If you want to learn more, there is a wealth of information at your fingertips and many books you can read on the subject.

The basic idea is to come up with a visual representation of an emotion, give it a name and a short back story. Don't focus solely on the negative stuff, as you will also want to be able to obtain the positive aspects of your personality quickly as well. You may well find that meditation and or a ritual process will help you to find your visual image or conjure a back story.

As an illustration, I will tell you about one of mine. He is called Charbon, and he represents my fear. I see him as a huge scribbled figure in black with no face and a body similar to 'The Hulk'. He can emerge from the shadows at any point and attack me from behind. I get no warning of his approach, except, perhaps, a vague feeling and just a glimpse of him in the corner of my eye beforehand. He has popped up on a few occasions during meditations.

However, it was once in a dream when I woke with a smile that I realised how to defeat him. In the dream, Charbon appeared in the corner of a room, and I was struck with fear. I shifted my gaze to reveal a small boy playing with an action figure on the opposite side of the room. I realised Charbon was just the huge shadow from the boy's little toy projected onto the wall by the light from a torch laying on the floor, and if I removed the torch, the big thing I feared became something trivial: a child's plaything. Therefore, if I treated my fears in the same way a child fearlessly plays with their toys, then fear would not hold power over me. A common phrase heard in AA that I appreciate: "It's not the mountains that trip you up, it's the molehills", reminds me that it's the small things that cause us more problems than those that seem much bigger.

ASPECTS OF SELF THAT CAN BE TAPPED INTO

Now that I have my own aspects of self that I can go to, I have created a system that I can tap into whenever and where ever I like. I found this difficult at first, but the final phase of this process made things surprisingly easy in the end, although it's been quite a journey to get here!

Finally, I went through a process of creating sigils for each of these characters. I did this so I could banish them (more an acknowledgement and shrinking of their importance) or invoke them, as and when I need to, with the power of a symbol. This enables me to have a faster way to manipulate my feelings and emotions: to provide the best outcome for me without using substances.

Again I'm not going to take you through this process. If you feel that it is something that will be of benefit to you, then you can look up Sigil magick for yourself. I'd also recommend that you take a quick look at chaos magick while you are there too.

---

[1] The Twelve Steps of Alcoholics Anonymous. (n.d.). Retrieved from http://www.aa.org/assets/en_US/smf-121_en.pdf

XX

FRIENDSHIP CIRCLES

I'll cut right to the chase with this one, these will change, and they need to for the better.

> "Learning from abstinent role models and using them to help support abstinence is a very effective strategy and lies at the heart of mutual self-help approaches, such as Alcoholics Anonymous or Narcotics Anonymous. Professional approaches, such as social network and behaviour therapy, aim to build support for behaviour change amongst family and friends. This support network may help protect individuals from the negative influence of substance-using friends, as well as providing rewarding social activities to fill the time that used to be spent using drugs or alcohol. Family and network approaches have the added advantage of potentially reducing

the stressful burden placed on those close to
a dependent substance user."

– Dr Ed Day[2]

I still have a very small close group of people that I call
my friends and an even smaller group that have been
with me through the drinking days and are still with
me now; this is of my own choosing, and these people
know who they are.

It was this group of friends who were the ones that I
told about my AA attendance a few weeks after I had
gone to my first meeting and, apart from my wife, they
were the first to know I was in the process of stopping
drinking for good. I didn't want to make a big thing
of going to AA, and I didn't want the whole world to
know until I was ready to tell them.

My wife obviously took most of the strain from my
drinking and also my recovery. She has been absolutely
amazing and still is, despite my occasional moody
days and sudden mood changes when really random
things can set off my irritability. My close friends
were brilliant and actually made my recovery process
a lot easier than it could have been: by backing me up
when I needed it, understanding that I might need to
leave early from a night out and generally looking out
for me.

There were also, of course, the arseholes that I used
to call friends. Once their regular manipulation tools
failed to get me to drink and use, they would go on the

attack in an attempt to get what they wanted; to get the only thing that mattered to them: a partner in crime. What I quickly found with these people was that we used each other and, apart from the drink or drugs, we had very little in common except the places we had been.

[1] Overview of treatment approaches – ugc.futurelearn.com. (n.d.). Retrieved from https://ugc.futurelearn.com/uploads/files/.../Overview_of_t reatment_approaches.pdf

[2] Dr Ed Day, Senior Clinical Lecturer in Addiction Psychiatry, King's College, London.

XXI

BUZZ THEORY
TO S-THEORY

OK, I'll start off by explaining the Buzz Theory and then how that adapts into the S-Theory and by what means that can be utilised to its greatest effect.

When you first start out using drugs and alcohol, typically you'll just have a few pints or cans of beer/cider, a puff on a friend's cigarette or spliff and this will give you the desired buzz you're looking for at the time. It's exciting and new, the feelings all rush at you at once and this thrilling experience is what you will ultimately spend the rest of your days trying to recreate.

Of course, the initial dosage only works for a short time before you will need to increase the amount necessary to get the same buzz. You'll then keep on increasing doses until you find that these substances no longer do it for you. So, then, you move on to the harder substances, for example, you move from the beer or cider to spirits and from the class C/B drugs to the class A stuff.

Then further down this road, you'll reach the stage where you have worked out a personal system, of using set drinks and drugs in the correct combinations, to obtain the desired buzz you're after. You'll know, for example, that you need a line of coke midway through the night to keep you awake so you can drink more. You need that hit of MDMA to help you to socialise, so you are not alone. You need that stashed bottle of vodka in your coat to get you home at the end of the night, so your alcohol levels don't drop. You need that stashed bottle of whisky when you get home so you can pass out and don't smash up your flat.

You see, you and your addiction have evolved together to get you to a point where you have found the optimum efficiency to get the buzz you require. This multi-layered pattern of behaviour, which can continuously evolve, has become your Model Dependent Reality (MDR), your theoretical way to achieve a buzz, in other words, your Buzz Theory. In my opinion, to attempt to defeat this ever-evolving Buzz Theory and maintain that successfully for an extended period is doomed to failure using just a single-layered solution based on a belief in God. Relying just on the Christian God, like your starter substance, will only get you so far before it no longer works.

You need to find a system that is adaptable and can evolve with you in the same way your addiction has.

A system that can overlap groups of ideas to give you an alternative MDR structure to the one you had to support you when using in your addicted state. You know this multi-layered approach already works because you've tested it with your using and are familiar how it functions, so now you can apply that hard-won knowledge to your recovery process.

I found the system in S-Theory[1] and the 90% 10% Thinking[2] of Rational Satanism.

To help understand the multi-layered structure, let's consider some definitions:

* **System** – a set of things working together as parts of an interconnecting network; a complex whole.

  In our system, these 'things' are ideas that we have researched which can include straightforward concepts and more complex theories:

* **Concept** – an abstract idea.

* **Theory** – a supposition or a system of ideas intended to explain something, especially one based on general principles independent of the thing to be explained.

* **Supposition** – a belief held without proof or certain knowledge; an assumption or hypothesis.

So in simple terms, S-Theory can be described as a grouping of already established ideas working in harmony to allow the individual to achieve the optimum performance from their MDR and everyday life. Similarly, their MDR can be described simply as 'how they see the world'.

This collection of ideas can contain anything from simple concepts to theories that encompass belief systems, philosophical principles and scientific theories.

A successful system needs to contain ideas that overlap so that they can work together in harmony within a complex whole. It also needs to be able to adapt to significant changes in understanding brought about by a paradigm shift. These are important topics and will be discussed in more detail later.

So how does this work and how do you develop your recovery S-Theory to best fit your needs?

It was described by one affiliate:

> "Like trying to explain how your personal style would suit someone else. People really do need to read and understand and then make it their own."

What I will do is explain the process and how I have crafted my own personal style and give you examples of how I apply it to give you a few ideas of how to craft your own. And for some strange reason, I now feel a bit like the fashion guru Gok Wan!! So hopefully you won't finish this book with the satanic equivalent of a pencil skirt and a large belt!

On the following pages, I will take you through a brief description of how S-Theory works.

The great thing about Satanism is the way we craft our views of reality; we have many tools to evaluate situations (as we have already discovered) and paint the clearest personal picture we can.

We can't afford to limit ourselves to one view and take one system as absolute. From investigating and delving into our sources, we should be able to come up with multiple "what if" theories: candidates that might work together. The easiest way to check if a theory will work and mould into a viable system is to look for overlapping points.

What you are looking for here is elegance, an affinity, a sympathetic relationship, between theories and ideas so that they can work together. You want to avoid the need to butcher a new theory, alter it to a significant degree, just so that it can fit with your current system. It has to have overlap with things you already know and understand, and if replacing a previous theory, it should achieve results at least as good if not better than you found before. From this process, you are creating a new model of reality, your **Model Dependent Reality (MDR)**, and sticking with the fashion theme, you are essentially picking an elegant outfit that matches so no suit and running trainers!

You can draw from various sources: Science, Religion, Gnostic texts and on and on; the list is endless.

So strutting its stuff on the catwalk, here I give you my 2016 summer collection of S-Theory overlapping theories that make up my MDR:

On a serious note, I came to the realisation of my own multi-layered recovery system while sitting in an AA meeting before I'd even read the Rational Satanism books which explained S-Theory and, once discovered, I was delighted to find a like-minded philosophy.

Not wanting to bow down to a Christian God, I had found a connection with the polytheist's idea of Odinism. It appealed to me because these gods were never shown without their faults and so I found them more human. This led me to think of the people at the meeting I was in as manifestations of the Norse gods. My thoughts progressed to consider my friends instead of these strangers and then further to break it down into aspects of my own personality.

So I then found myself in the meeting sitting at the head of the table on my throne surrounded by the different aspects of my personality. So here is an illustration of where the overlaps in my theory fit together and function to give me the best system that works for me.

It allows me to mix Satanism, Odinism, runes, Jung's theories like shadow work, demonology, occult practices, chaos magick, alchemy, symbology, sigil crafting, maths, science, art, psychology and philosophy to name but a few.

As you can see S-Theory is the basis for the individual's MDR by simply looking for overlapping points to create a model that works for you. Another way to understand this is discussed with the 'holes in the wall' example from the book S-Theory:[1]

If you imagine a wall with holes or openings in it, you can only see part of what is on the other side. For the areas between the holes you cannot see, you will have to imagine the overlap so that your mind can visualise the whole. Different people will construct the overlap in a variety of ways using their objective reality to make the connection. This process would also apply to constructing a viable overlap between candidate theories.

This is similar to what visual effects people do to join images together. If any of you saw The Marble and Granite – Antithesis of Sarcophagi garden from the RHS Chelsea Flower show you would have a practical example of how this works. The garden was grown inside a 10ft granite block where it was only visible through several small holes. What the viewers of the garden had to do was to overlap what they saw to create an overall image of the garden inside.

Like with all models, they can change and evolve as another overlapping philosophical principle becomes evident.

S-Theory is creating a model that has set rules from your knowing and connects the elements of your observations; this is advantageous to anyone who has a higher subjective fraction of the 90% 10% Thinking concept, as they already make the subjective objective, by the results they discover. To add that to S-Theory it would be a sum like this:

Subjectivity + Observations x results = MDR

And this is your subjective sum.

From this model created using S-Theory, the subjective workings have been observed then multiplied by the results to produce a theory of success, which is sufficiently robust to overlap with the model of reality that is being lived by. This strengthens the system and allows for the model to be given validity by the individual.

Validating this equation brings us nicely on to the topic of 'Theorising' itself and to do this we use what every satanic superhero needs, a utility belt or more importantly, in this case, 'The Cognitive Utility Belt'.

You may hear many people claim that "knowledge is power". This statement is, at best, both a boastful and shallow claim. Knowledge can only be considered truly powerful if the person knew everything. Otherwise, there will always be someone who knows something you don't, rendering your knowledge "powerless".

Knowledge is just a tool to help us advance, but it makes up part of a three piece utility that we carry around with us every day. This set consists of knowledge, wisdom and insight.

The application of all three elements are a vital part of theory making and reaching logical conclusions, but they also apply to all the everyday matters that we have to deal with as individuals.

S-Theory is a combination of all three of these tools; it's an infinite model to theorise and pull the deeper meaning of knowing to fit into your reality. To simplify theory creating, we can put it to three categories:

Hypothesise, **Investigate** and **Results**.

Now if you look into those three aspects of theorising then you can see where each element is an internal cognitive tool of theory creating.

The **Hypothesise** aspect relates to **Knowledge**.

The **Investigative** aspect relates to **Wisdom**.

And finally, the **Results** aspect relates to **Insight**.

This again shows how S-theory can create a stronger model of reality as the deeper meaning in knowledge acquired will always be found through referring to your S-theory model. This allows you to see where your wisdom and insight will allow your results to overlap.

So if we consider again 'the holes in the wall' example with the restricted view of reality, then you should be able to see that what is visible is knowledge, and the overlapping part of your perception is your wisdom and insight that make up your MDR.

Knowledge alone doesn't bring power; it's simply a tool that makes part of a set; when you add wisdom and insight it does bring power, but that is only power for the self to excel and it will be used in your reality as you see fit.

So to conclude things now, we are going to look at Paradigm Shifting. As you've seen demonstrated one of the most likened attributes to Rational Satanism, is its adaptability.

I find what works best for me and use it until I have a paradigm shift.

The term 'paradigm shift' was first identified by the American physicist and philosopher Thomas Kuhn (1922–1996), and can be defined as a fundamental change or 'revolution' in the basic concepts of a scientific discipline. This concept can also work from a philosophical viewpoint, and the success of your MDR depends on your ability to see the exact same thing in a completely different way by changing your perspective.

Your system will typically have been crafted from theories you would have studied over years.

A paradigm shift shouldn't be confused, however, with a complete change in ideology.

You are simply going to alter your MDR views, by using S-Theory, where you see changes that need to be made.

When such a significant change in my understanding occurs, it allows me then to remove aspects that no longer work and replace them with new concepts after I have taken them through the subjective sum (the equation used to validate changes to the system discussed previously).

This keeps my recovery moving forward; it allows me to keep my ideas fresh and exciting and makes the recovery process fit and adapt to how I work as an individual.

Looking at it another way, when a paradigm shift occurs: what the anomalies may cause are holes within the model itself, these holes require that portion of S-Theory not to be replaced but added to and adapted with a more viable theory. This change is made attainable by utilising the dimensions and realms found within the system, which are described in more detail below.

The cognitive realms aspect of analysing and creating your S-Theory derives from using some of the 8 Cognitive Realms of Existence; the dimensions allocated within S-Theory are the three scientific dimensions of the XYZ axis.

These are the fundamental make-up of the objective perception: length, width (or height) and depth, where:

✷ Length is the X axis
✷ Width is the Y axis
✷ Depth is the Z axis

Here the XYZ axis would relate to realms 2, 3 and 4 of the 8 Cognitive Realms of Existence, which are, of course, Knowledge, Comprehension and Analysis (which utilises the 90% 10% Thinking^2 concept).

If you imagine creating a 3D graph model, where the points relate to the three different coordinates, then these are your 'holes in the wall', the lines or web that link these up are your S-Theory, and these create your MDR. And, as you can see, this web idea links in well with the runes and the Web of Wyrd as well as satisfying my more scientific side as it is consistent with the chaos butterfly theory.

So a paradigm shift would be where one of these points moved slightly within the graph or web. This change would happen from gaining new pieces of knowledge, gaining a better understanding of the knowledge you already had or moving something from the 10% fraction to the 90% of vice versa.

Knowledge (including wisdom and insight) and the quest for it is obviously a major part of the satanic system.

S-Theory cannot be attained without knowledge gained, which is aimed towards your model of reality. Many forms of knowledge will have been gathered to create your base fraction (the 90%) and S-Theory model. You would have explored many different systems and taken from them what fits your MDR.

This knowledge realm is constantly expanding and improving the self. If through science you can give attributes that are knowing (i.e. from Realm 2 – Knowledge), and have empirical values; you can create quite an objectively based S-Theory that will adapt and cover the gaps that have arisen in your model.

Even though what you are gathering from the XYZ axis doesn't make objective sense you can make a conclusion that fits with your MDR.

Knowledge and comprehension are aspects of our reality that help us create our worldview and ultimately our S-Theory MDR.

Hopefully, you have gained an appreciation of how S-Theory can help support your recovery from the overview in this chapter, but if anything is still unclear, there is obviously far more detailed knowledge available in the book[1].

[1] Banks, Lee. (n.d.). "Rational Satanism S-Theory by CoRS Merchandising." CoRS. Retrieved from http://corsmerch.tictail.com/product/rational-satanism-s- theory

[2] 90% 10% Thinking. (n.d.). Retrieved from http://www. churchofrationalsatanism.com/essays/90-10- thinking/

STEP 7

HUMBLY ASKED HIM TO REMOVE
OUR SHORTCOMINGS.[1]

Just because you now know how to 'drive the car' does not make you a good driver! So don't beat yourself up when you make a mistake: learn from it and work on it; store the data in your 'godhead' files, so you know for next time. Return to the 'godhead' and seek the power to manage the extremes of character just as you sought the power to eliminate the obsession to drink.

To do this, you are going to have to look at the "What should I have done" column, as this is going to be the basis for your plan of action. You are looking to lay out a way to remove the patterns you perceive as being negative and damaging to your vital existence and removing them.

This will not be an easy task, and you will not change overnight, you are fighting against years of self-programming. Initially, just being able to spot when a behaviour pattern is emerging is going to be a big step; this is you becoming more self-aware. Once you can see the patterns and have an understanding of the most likely end result, based on your previous experience, you can make a more informed choice as to whether you want to change its course, or not, for a more desired outcome.

With this new perspective of yourself, you should be able to take responsibility for the things that surfaced and stop negative cycles from reoccurring. I'm sure, when you look in detail, there were a lot of times when the satanic sins came up that you hadn't previously noticed and times when you were convinced you were right when, in fact, you were wrong.

This part of the process is also a test phase. You'll find that sometimes when you have followed the "What should I have done?" section, from Step 4, you may not get the desired outcome you are looking for, and so will need to tweak the actions taken to get the outcome you want. Don't worry, this will take time, and you are not always going to get there the first time around. You may also find that you know exactly what to do to stop a chain of events from occurring, but the self- programming is so ingrained, that it felt like all you could do was sit back and watch as the chaos unfolded.

You have to go to your godhead or archetype with some form of humility, as you have not managed to attain a perfect likeness to it yet because you are still at a learning stage. You are still in the process of self-discovery and remodelling.

[1] The Twelve Steps of Alcoholics Anonymous. (n.d.). Retrieved from http://www.aa.org/assets/en_US/smf-121_en.pdf

XXII

THE OLD WOMAN WHO SWALLOWED A FLY

Hopefully, you remember the children's story, which was originally a song "I Know an Old Lady".[1]

If you don't, it goes a little something like this:

> There was an old lady who swallowed a fly;
>
> I don't know why she swallowed a fly –
>
> perhaps she'll die!
>
> There was an old lady who swallowed a spider;
>
> That wriggled and jiggled and tickled inside her!
>
> She swallowed the spider to catch the fly;
>
> I don't know why she swallowed a fly –
>
> perhaps she'll die!
>
> ...

She continues to swallow increasingly large animals, in the hope that the next one will kill the previous one, until inevitably and I'm sorry if it spoils the story for you: she dies!

This story could easily be the plot for my drinking. I'd have a few drinks, and I'd do something stupid. The next day I'd regret the stupid thing but act like it hadn't bothered me. The only way I knew how to hide my emotions was to drink again: only this time, I'd need a little bit more. The progression would then lead me to make a bigger mistake in a continuing escalating cycle.

From the outside, as with the story, it's really stupid to be like the old lady, but when you are the old lady, it seems like the only logical answer to the problem. Inevitably, though, the problem solver is also the problem maker.

[1] "I Know an Old Lady." copyrighted in 1952. The song was written by Rose Bonne (lyrics) and Canadian folk artist Alan Mills (Albert Miller)

XXIII

USING = FUN?

One of the major issues I had, when I stopped drinking at the age of 24, was the problem of having that feeling of despair as to how I was meant to have fun without drinking or drugs.

Due to my drinking, I had developed a connection between fun and having to drink. Therefore, I was going to have to find a new way to "have fun" without a drink. Of course, in those dark days near the end, not much fun was had while drinking, but the connection still remained.

Not only did achieving this goal feel like a daunting task, but it also ended up being very hit and miss. In the beginning, it did require lots of planning, as I was never quite sure how I was going to react in different situations since they were all new. After a while of testing things out, with some great successes and a few near misses, I found out the best ways for me to deal with them.

Most of my planning was for an 'escape route' from an event and making sure I was with understanding friends who would be OK with me having to duck out early. If I knew there would be people drinking at an event, I would make sure to get there early and leave early so as not to be exposed to others in a drunken state. Although being sober and seeing people off their faces is an excellent way to see what a twat I must have been while drunk!

Feelings of discomfort, anxiety and depression are normal in these situations, and during recovery in general, as they are related to change. In general, people fear the unknown and your brain is trying its hardest to return to its 'default setting'. It is striving to go back to the behavioural pathways that have become entrenched after you have spent so many years 'perfecting' them. It's only outside of your comfort zone, past the fear, that the magic happens. It's not a beast or the devil but 'learnt behaviour' that you feel comfortable with; that will take time to rewire.

One thing that helps to lock in new behaviours is a reward system. If you reward yourself for good behaviour, then you are more likely to repeat the same action. After, say, a week or so of not drinking, for example, I used the money I had saved to buy myself a new record and then put the rest to good use, either to pay off debts or to add to a savings jar for a bigger reward.

I will admit that I do, on occasion, smoke weed at social events, but it's very little and only once or twice a year maximum. The main reason many in AA will frown upon this is that it is a common weakness for people to swap their addictive substances. Individuals will react differently to substances, so you need to be mindful and aware of how it affects you. For me, I can pick up and leave marijuana without any issues, having a small amount around does not give me a craving for it, and I can go quite happily for a year knowing that I have a small amount. I do not get into the same out of control states with it, and so, for me, it is a personal choice. In my early recovery, it was helpful at large events to take the edge off my feelings for drinking. Nevertheless, I'm only talking about weak joints and about two a day maximum while at a 3-day music festival and then only in social situations. This also doesn't mean that I'm not able to be at these events while completely sober and I have done that as well. If I were to find that I had a compulsion for this substance, I would do something about it.

I was a light to medium smoker from the age of 17, and on my second attempt, I was able to stop smoking after fifteen years, nearly cold turkey, and have no desire to go back to it. I did it by using a psychological trick on myself to allow me to quit smoking without a problem. My AA sponsor told me that nicotine only takes 72 hours out of the system for your body not to crave it; after that, it is just the habit that causes you to smoke again.

With this in mind, I spent two weeks before I quit changing my smoking habits; I would try to last that little bit longer after eating, or the kids had gone to bed, to have a cigarette. During this 2- week period, I would also chew menthol chewing gum after each time. This gave my brain the connection between nicotine and mint, or menthol, gum. I then bought a menthol e- cigarette, with the intention of using this for a short while to decrease the nicotine slowly, but I ended up only using it for 24 hours. After which, every time I felt like I wanted to have a cigarette I would have a menthol gum, and then I would go and do something to occupy my mind and my hands if I could.

I also cut out sugar in my tea and coffee at the same time because I figured, if I was going to be ratty without smoking, I might as well add that in, and if there was something that I didn't mind going back to, the sugar was less important than the smoking. The impetus to stop smoking was for the arrival of my son. I'm happy to report that, other than the odd sugar in a chai tea, I have refrained from both since 1st March 2015.

STEP 8 AND STEP 9

MADE A LIST OF ALL PERSONS WE HAD HARMED, AND BECAME WILLING TO MAKE AMENDS TO THEM ALL.[1]

Along our way, through addiction and into recovery we would have done things we are not proud of and maybe unintentionally stomped on a few people. The best way to stop these things from affecting us in our daily lives is by dealing with them head on.

MADE DIRECT AMENDS TO SUCH PEOPLE WHEREVER POSSIBLE, EXCEPT WHEN TO DO SO WOULD INJURE THEM OR OTHERS.[1]

If you know someone or something is going to cause more aggro by you going to see them or trying to fix the situation, then just let it go.

I have put these two steps together as they are quite self-explanatory really; you would have found out if you hadn't already realised, that some people along the way would have been unintentionally harmed either physically or psychologically. I would suggest that you only try to rectify those situations that are damaging to your own vital existence, which you should have identified while doing Steps 4 and 5.

Obviously, going to try and make amends to someone when you know that it will have an adverse effect, possibly psychologically damaging for them, will be of no benefit to them. It may make you feel better for a short while but, no doubt in time, it will come back to bite you on the arse.

---

[1] The Twelve Steps of Alcoholics Anonymous. (n.d.). Retrieved from http://www.aa.org/assets/en_US/smf-121_en.pdf

XXIV

Relapse and Power of Suggestion

Relapses can and do happen, but they don't have to. The point is, if they do, they don't have to be the end of the world or the end or your recovery. Many will see relapse as a failure, but it's usually just a sign that your system is not working in the best way possible for you. If we look again at the 9 satanic mnemonics, described in the chapter 'La Porte de l'Enfer' and further explained in Rational Satanism Futureproof Adaptability[1], the seventh mnemonic has 7 steps, of which the 4th step defines failure as:

> "Failure – you may feel this is a strange step to put in, but it's as equally important as the rest. No one can go through life without failing at some point. What the Satanist needs to do is learn from it, don't dwell on it, use the perspective we have to bounce back stronger

> with a safeguarding technique in place, so it doesn't happen again. You may not have achieved your desired objective, but now it's simply a case of redoing the maths and coming to a pragmatic plan of action while not taking the thoughts of your failure with you. Failure does not mean you're completely unsuccessful; it's simply a learning curve."

If we look at the Church of Satan's 'Satanic Sins'[2], there are more than half with the potential to take us directions we didn't really want to go that can lead us to relapse, for example, Solipsism, Self-deceit, Lack of Perspective, Counterproductive Pride and Lack of Aesthetics.

Another thing we should try not to do is overload your system with too much information in one go, trying to do too much and not allowing things to take their own time to sink in and be properly processed. Too much information will get jumbled up if it doesn't have the appropriate outlet or before you can fully process it.

There is a great YouTube video that describes this process really well. You can find it under the title 'Mystery School Lesson 14: Even Flow'. In the video, Frater Xavier talks about the need for balance stating that: "too much coming in and not enough going out creates blockages and in reverse too much going out with not enough coming in and you will deplete yourself very quickly". He goes on to talk about cluttering up the mind and how trying to keep things like calendar dates in your mind creates mental blocks, and this is why it's important to write stuff down.

Personally, I write loads of stuff down. I currently have a ring-binder folder dedicated to my recovery and another one devoted to the Church of Rational Satanism (CoRS) as well as three notepads and a notebook app on my phone! I find it most helpful when your brain is racing, and you can't get to sleep at night or when I keep replaying a situation in my head. I write it down and get rid of it. If it's something that I permanently want to eradicate, I will use the symbolic approach of either throwing it in the bin, burning it or tying it to a balloon and letting that go. Writing stuff down will also free up space for you to concentrate on other things, think clearer and process things faster.

In the same YouTube video, Frater Xavier goes on to use some great examples of when you try to go from one polar extreme to another, and from an addiction to recovery perspective, you can see why I liked them. In his first example he talks about weather fronts, and when a hot front reaches a cold front you get a storm, and when you put boiling water into a cold glass, it shatters. He's saying you can't go from one extreme to the other or in magical terms "you can't go from one polar extreme to the other too quickly, or it will be destructive" it has to be a gradual process.

My favourite bit in the video is his metaphor of the goldfish in the bag waiting for the water to reach the correct temperature because if it released into the tank or pond water too early, it will get sick and die. So don't rush, let things take their time, remember if you are after long- term recovery it's a marathon and not a sprint. You don't have to know everything right from the get-go; you should build on the foundations you have, add new information when you learn it and let your system evolve with you.

In my opinion, this next topic highlights the two main causes for people to relapse, and that's negative suggestions and response expectancies. If you've ever had someone tell you that a dental or medical procedure "will really hurt," or that a test "will be very hard," or that a new boss "is impossible to deal with" and then those scenarios have played out just as predicted . It's because those early suggestions probably shaped your reality[3].

A deliberate suggestion can influence how you remember things, how you respond to them, and even how well you will perform and behave[4]. So if someone keeps telling you, or more importantly you keep telling yourself that a recovery treatment you are on will fail it more than likely will. The reason for this is attributable to something called **response expectancies**[3]. Meaning the way we anticipate our response to a given situation actually influences how we will respond to it[3]. In other words, once you expect something to happen, your behaviours, thoughts, and reactions will actually contribute to making that expectation occur[3] which can be used in both a positive and negative way.

Using suggestion in this way can be a powerful tool in accomplishing our goals[3]. If you think you'll win a race, for example, you're more likely to train, prepare, and perform in a way that gives you a greater chance of victory[3]. But many of us get caught up thinking only of their limitations. The power of suggestion is just as powerful in those situations to actually sabotaging our success[3] as it is to help us gain success in the first place.

Therefore negative suggestion is something that really should be avoided as much as possible especially in recovery. It works by the subconscious part of the mind ignoring the negation terms such as no, not, avoid, stop and so on. For example, the suggestion that 'avoid drink' is liable to be taken as 'drink'. At best, this will simply confirm a behaviour you are all too aware of; however, worst of all, it will encourage the very problem you are seeking to avoid, and because of this negative thought process you may actually be unconsciously doing things to sabotage your own recovery.

This is where contradictory impulses seem to arise when people focus intensely on avoiding specific errors or taboos. The theory is straightforward: for example, to avoid blurting out an insult, the brain must first imagine just that; the very presence of that catastrophic insult, in turn, increases the odds that the brain will spit it out[5]. The risk that people will slip or "lose it" and relapse depends in part on the level of stress they are undergoing. There can also come a certain relief "from just getting it over with, having that worst thing happen, so you don't have to worry about monitoring it anymore.[6]"

To convert a negative suggestion to a positive one you will need to ask yourself 'how do you want to be?' In the case of addiction, you obviously want to be free from your substance. Thus a Positive Suggestion will say something like, 'You enjoy your recovery', or 'You now have a sober view of life'.

If you are still unsure maybe use one of the following:

You allow yourself to enjoy being in recovery/sober
You have a confidence about life in recovery
You enjoy meeting people for a coffee and a chat
Relax and let go

You can use the power of suggestion right now, though, to create the experiences you desire in your own life[3] and your recovery. First of all, you need to have an awareness of the moment as this is required to help you identify the types of suggestions that are coming your way in the first place. If you are not aware of the messages you're sending or receiving from others, it's tough to counteract the negative suggestions you hear[3].

Once you have become aware of the types of suggestions, you'll need to create a support network. By identifying the people that believe in you and staying close to them, you will pick up on their positive suggestions, as we are influenced by deliberate and non-deliberate suggestion. How people interact with you, their gestures, tones, and implications matter just as much as what they say[3]. These subtle suggestions can either build people up and inspire them, or tear them down, all without you saying a word. Positive influence generates positive suggestions, so think about who you spend the most time with. I touch more on this in the chapter on friendship circles.

You'll also need to maintain a flexible mind-set, and this is where the paradigm shifting aspect of the Rational Satanism system really comes in handy. When you are locked into a fixed mind-set, you will tend to take failure personally and see little opportunity for improvement[3], which is very limiting. With flexible thinking, we can continue to learn, grow, improve, and draw things into our life that will influence our progress[3].

Lastly, you need to understand that the power of suggestion is always working. If you expect something to happen, your expectations of that outcome will play a major role in its occurrence. The expectation or suggestion alone, often unconsciously, changes your behaviour and your responses to help bring into reality the outcome you are expecting.[3]

Knowing all this, don't expect anything less than the best. I suggest that you deserve it![3]

I followed a similar psychological approach when I eventually stopped smoking. I first discussed this in the chapter 'Using=Fun?' but below is a more detailed description so you can see how the power of suggestion worked for me when I applied it successfully in the end.

I was told by my AA sponsor that the body only craves nicotine for 72 hours and once you are past this point, then it is just the habit of smoking, and the negative suggestion of not smoking that encourages you to get back in the habit. I had quit once before when my daughter was born so we could co-sleep and I did this cold turkey. Unfortunately, I returned to smoking again just five months later, after a traumatic event unsettled my resolve when I had to put the cat down. Although for the next three months I would only have one cigarette a day (in the evening in the garden after my daughter had been put to bed).

Fast forward two and a half years to when the arrival of my son was announced and, although my daughter had only seen me smoke twice, I was back up to 10-15 rollies a day (roll your own cigarettes).

So I set myself a deadline of stopping at least a month before my son was due to be born. To do this, I incorporated a psychological approach including the power of suggestion and devised a 4-fold plan. Break the habit, reduce the nicotine intake, commit to memory and then stop for good.

To start with I spent two to three weeks breaking my routine cigarettes. By this I mean the smoke after food or with a coffee, the one before picking up the kids or the one after the kids went to bed. To start with, I would see if I actually felt like I wanted a cigarette, then when I got the urge, I would see how long I could push it before I gave in. What I found with the technique was that it actually meant I was cutting down at the same time.

One of the big issues with pre-rolled cigarettes is the idea of not wanting to waste a whole one. However, the tobacco companies are clever, and they designed them to give you a bigger hit than you need meaning you will always crave more. So the trick when trying to quit is just to take that initial hit and stub it out, or if you roll your own, use less tobacco or smaller papers. Changing papers may also help as different weights of papers will actually go out by themselves.

I also decided to add in a little bit of magic in the form of a memory recognition technique to see if it would work. Every time I had a cigarette, I would have a menthol chewing gum. This allowed my brain to make the connection between the menthol flavour and the nicotine hit. The next stage in the reduction was to get a menthol e-cig and then use that when I got the craving as well as using the chewing gum.

I ended up only using the e-cig for a grand total of 24 hours taking about 8-10 puffs from it. In that period, I then went cold turkey knowing that I would only need to last 72 hours without any nicotine in my system from the e-cig, but it was there if I needed it as a comfort blanket. Whenever I got the need to have a cigarette, I would have a chewing gum to trick the brain into thinking I'd had a nicotine hit thanks to the memory recognition I put in place for myself.

I would also couple the chewing gum with finding something for my brain to do as well as my hands a Sudoku puzzle is a good suggestion; however, if you can do something that involves a physical activity at the same time, even better, as it will reduce your stress levels at the same time. This also stopped me negatively suggesting the idea of a cigarette and gave me something constructive to do.

I'm pleased to say that I've not had a cigarette since 1st March 2015, as planned before my son was born.

A quick point to add in this section, before I finish up, was a result of an argument I got into with someone who was very anti- AA, to the point that they couldn't see anyone being able to find the system useful despite my constant presentation of evidence to the contrary. However, this person did mention something of value: Logotherapy[7]. I did some brief research and found that it could be a very useful addition to anyone's recovery system and will work alongside the AA programme without any problems at all. Developed by Viktor Frankl, the theory is founded on the belief that human nature is motivated by the search for a life purpose; logotherapy is the pursuit of that meaning for one's life8 and to focus on the things you enjoy. I won't go into the theory too much, but I would definitely suggest looking into it.

So let's finish this chapter off with Drinking dreams or Relapse dreams. I felt I really needed to add this because as result of writing this chapter I ended up having one! It is quite common to have an occasional relapse dream or drinking dream in recovery, this is where you experience using alcohol or drugs, so if you do have, one you don't need to worry. These can be enjoyable; however, they can also be quite alarming, confusing and can leave you quite shaken. One dream

I had was so vivid I had to ask my wife and phone the friend that was in my dream to confirm that the situation hadn't happened!! So as you can imagine you could wake with a sense of euphoria or as if you've come from a nightmare. This can affect your mood for the whole day if you let it and it is also why some people in recovery have concluded that they are an omen to relapse; but with the power of suggestion we have learnt already in this chapter, we understand why that is and how we can stop it.

It is important that you realise that such dreams are a normal part of recovery and that they may even be a positive occurrence, reminding you of the stuff you don't have to go through any more or the fact you've woken up with a clear head. In some instances though, these dreams may be a sign that people need to put more focus back into their recovery, but only you can be the judge of that.

There are a number of reasons why relapse dreams may occur; as addicts, these substances would have been a major part of our lives, so it is understandable that these memories will influence our dreams. It may also be the case that the dream was inspired by random events that occurred that day or individuals that triggered these subconscious thoughts which often associate drinking or using with reward or pleasure. Therefore because of this, you are more likely to have these dreams when you are going through stressful times in your life, and they are good indicators that you need to look for better ways of coping with situations.

As previously stated, it is up to you, the individual, to act or react to the dreams as you see fit and evaluate a meaning from them. You can then decide, from that conclusion, what you do with them: speak with someone, write it down and let it go or make changes to your recovery system if you feel something is not quite right. Remember though, it's just a dream, you haven't drunk or used drugs, and you can use it as a motivating factor to go in either a positive or negative direction, but it's ultimately you who is left with that choice.

[1] Banks, Lee. (n.d.). "Rational Satanism Futureproof Adaptability by CoRS Merchandising." CoRS, Web. Retrieved from http://corsmerch.tictail.com/product/rational- satanism-futureproof-adaptability

[2] LaVey, Anton S. (n.d.). The Nine Satanic Sins. Retrieved from http://www.churchofsatan.com/nine-satanic-sins.php

[3] 4 Ways the Power of Suggestion Can Change Your Life... (n.d.). Retrieved from https://www.psychologytoday.com/blog/imperfect-spirituality/201504/4-ways-the-power-suggestion-can- change-your-life

[4] The Power of Suggestion: What We Expect Influences Our Behavior, for Better or Worse. (n.d.). Retrieved from http://www.psychologicalscience.org/news/releases/the-power-of-suggestion-what-we-expect-influences-our-behavior-for-better-or-worse.html#.WPhefxiZNBw

[5] Why the Imp in Your Brain Gets Out – The New York Times. (n.d.). Retrieved from http://www.nytimes.com/2009/07/07/health/07mind.html

[6] Wegner, D. M. (2009, July 03). How to Think, Say, or Do Precisely the Worst Thing for Any Occasion. Retrieved from http://science.sciencemag.org/content/325/5936/48

[7] Viktor Frankl Institute of Logotherapy. (n.d.). Retrieved from http://www.logotherapyinstitute.org/About_Logotherapy.html

[8] Logotherapy. (n.d.). Retrieved from http://www.goodtherapy.org/learn-about-therapy/types/logotherapy

STEP 10

CONTINUED TO TAKE PERSONAL
INVENTORY AND WHEN WE WERE WRONG
PROMPTLY ADMITTED IT.[1]

You as an individual are constantly evolving; as a Satanist, you are constantly looking to learn new things, and your ideas will change over time; this will change how you view yourself, so it is important that you keep reviewing your own personal knowledge.

There are two things that I take from this sentence from a satanic perspective, and I will go through each separately. The first covers the beginning of the sentence "continued to take personal inventory", the second is the final part of the sentence "when we were wrong promptly admitted it".

So let's look at the first part, as I think this is an easy one, as it's the S-type personality that shines through here. The Satanist demand for study and not worship is what will serve him best here, that drive to be a better you tomorrow than you were yesterday but allowing yourself to completely live in the now.

To understand more about this personality we need to explore the satanic mind-set, which is a naturally consistently evolving one. Rational Satanism was designed to evolve with the individual, "as different ideologies come to make a pragmatic part of a personal satanic paradigm." Satanism effectively moves at a rate that you want it to. Rational Satanism is not here to school but simply be a representation of the adaptable progression of Satanism.

Self-evolution and development are sadly not going to happen to the human race naturally, and we consider it limited to individuals that only have the S-type personality. A heightened awareness of the world and natural abilities to see things from another perspective are satanically evolved aspects that you already own, but even these can grow to personally, rationally and pragmatically better the self.

You could say evolution to the Rational Satanist is attaining the pragmatic maxim. This is a vast forming of logic constantly guiding our enlightened thought process to achieve the overall goal. People with this S-type personality will also already be using some of the aspects of the 9 satanic mnemonics, which I have touched on at various points throughout the book.

Personally, I think you can see the S-type personalities in people quite clearly as they are the ones that will ask questions, listen, research and then formulate their own ideas and opinions based on what they have studied and then ask more questions. They are the ones that have that drive to consistently know more. They are the ones that are confident in what they know yet understand there is so much more to learn.

I also think that Viktor Frankl's Logotherapy[2], as mentioned in the previous chapter, is particularly relevant here. "Logotherapy is based on the premise that the human person is motivated by a 'will to meaning', an inner pull to find a meaning in life."[2]

"Logotherapy focuses on the future"[3] and using optimism to turn "suffering into human achievement and accomplishment"[3] and "deriving from guilt the opportunity to change oneself for the better"[3].

Frankl's theories were heavily influenced by his personal experiences of suffering and loss in Nazi concentration camps, and so his positive message on overcoming even the most miserable circumstances is compelling for the recovering alcoholic.

The second half of the sentence is something that struck me on my first time of reading. It's a simple thing to do, but so many people will paint themselves into a corner through counterproductive pride and sheer stubbornness just because they will not admit that they are wrong.

It's something I employed early on in my recovery as it stopped loads of small arguments with my wife that otherwise would have escalated. I was also given some of the best advice before going to a big job interview that ran very much along the same lines as this "if you don't know how to do something just say you don't but that you are willing to learn".

[1] The Twelve Steps of Alcoholics Anonymous. (n.d.). Retrieved from http://www.aa.org/assets/en_US/smf-121_en.pdf

[2] Viktor Frankl Institute of Logotherapy. (n.d.). Retrieved from http://www.logotherapyinstitute.org/About_Logotherapy.h tml

[3] About Victor Frankl – Institute of Logotherapy. (n.d). Retrieved from http://www.logotherapyinstitute.org/About_Viktor_Frankl.html

XXV

THE JESUS EFFECT

If you are told to take prescribed medicine by a Doctor, GP or medical profession, then take it. There are some people in recovery groups that think because it may contain a drug, you are automatically going to become addicted to it, or you are in some way cheating your recovery. Bullshit, the same people may believe that because they have a Christian God in their life, they can heal the sick like Jesus, but they can't. What you are prescribed by a medical professional is none of their business so do not let anyone try to convince you otherwise. If you have concerns about what you are taking, I would recommend that you seek medical advice rather than listen to the opinions of a recovering drunk or drug addict.

I normally tell my GP that I have an allergy to Alcohol so that I'm not given stuff that may inadvertently affect my recovery. Ultimately, if you don't feel comfortable doing something, then seek help from a professional and maybe ask for an alternative that won't trigger your addictive thought patterns.

The same people, who preached about prescriptions in one of my AA groups, also advised me not to use mouthwash because it contained alcohol; I'm not drinking the stuff, and I didn't get a craving for it, so I palmed them off. I thought I'd try the alcohol-free mouthwash though and found that to be more like washing my mouth out with Foster's Lager than the stuff that contained the alcohol! So you heard it here first: you'll be able to spot the 'god squad' in your recovery groups by their bad breath!

In another AA meeting, someone else told me that apples ferment in the stomach, so I should stop eating apples! At this point, an old-timer turned to me and explained "the body needs alcohol in very small doses, you will never rid the body of alcohol because if the body needs it, it will make its own! Either that or you can just stop eating fruit forever, but I think there is another group for that called Fruits Anonymous!"

You will also come across those who disagree when people talk about seeking 'outside help', meaning that they have gone to see a therapist about some of the issues that may have arisen from doing the Step 4 work. Seeking professional advice should never be frowned upon, the fact of the matter is we are all in recovery for the sole purpose of overcoming the addictions we once had, and we should be supportive of those who seek professional help if they feel it is a better option for them.

You see everyone in recovery will try to offer you some advice, some of it's good, and some of it is utter shit. Sadly, it's your job to figure out what's what; however, in some cases, it's easy to judge. Also, some will not want you to take a particular medicine because they felt they were not allowed to or they had an issue with it. This prejudice goes back to the "it didn't work for me so it can't work for anyone" attitude. Don't try and live someone else's recovery for them.

It's no one else's recovery but yours and yours alone, so when people stick their nose into your business unasked remind them to focus on their own recovery rather than yours unless they believe you are so important to them, you've somehow become their 'higher power'.

XXVI

OCCULT SYMBOLISM OF THE AA LOGO

I think the logo of AA is something that's definitely worth taking a look at, especially as it's great ammo to fire at the "AA is a Christian programme" bigots!

> "The Circle and Triangle symbol has long been connected to the A.A. Fellowship. It was adopted as an official A.A. symbol at the International Convention in St. Louis in 1955, and from that point on was widely used in the Fellowship. In Alcoholics Anonymous Comes of Age, Bill Wilson's 1955 speech, in which he describes the adoption of the symbol, is printed:
>
> *"Above us floats a banner on which is inscribed the new symbol for A.A., a circle enclosing a triangle. The circle stands for the whole world of A.A., and the triangle stands*

for A.A.'s Three Legacies of Recovery, Unity, and Service. Within our wonderful new world, we have found freedom from our fatal obsession. That we have chose this particular symbol is perhaps no accident. The priests and seers of antiquity regarded the circle enclosing the triangle as a means of warding off the spirits of evil, and A.A.'s circle and triangle of Recovery, Unity, and Service has certainly meant all of that to us and much more."
(p. 139)

However, in the early '90s, it was decided to phase out the use of the Circle and Triangle symbol on its literature, letterhead and other material and in 1994 the General Service Conference resolved that the logo be discontinued on all Conference-approved literature. Despite this, the symbol is still associated with Alcoholics Anonymous and other kinds of 12-Step recovery fellowships and has a special meaning for AA members all over the world.[1]"

Now on to the occult history and meaning of the symbol. I think, first of all, we will need to consider the two primary symbols, the triangle and the circle, separately and then look at what they are representing as a whole.

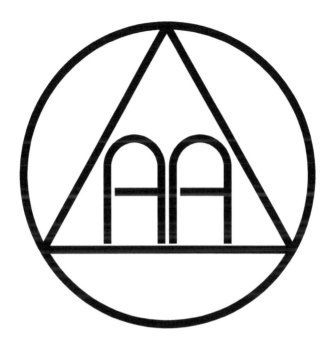

All symbols are said to be formed from variations of the dot and line or egg and sperm. The dot, line and circle are the most elementary of these. They are the parents from which all others have evolved. The dot, or point, signifies unity, the origin, source or beginning. The dot is obviously significant in the magical or ritual circle concept where the magician standing inside the protective circle becomes the dot. The circle, therefore, is the dot expanded to infinity, symbolising the universe, eternity, unity, eternal motion, the abyss and nothing.

The Circle is one of the most common and universal signs that can be found in all cultures. It is the symbol of the sun in its limitless or boundless aspect. It has no beginning or end, with no divisions, making it the perfect symbol of completeness, eternity and the soul. The circle is also the symbol of boundary, enclosure, of completion and returning cycles. The circle symbolism most familiar and significant to most of us is in the form of the wedding ring. It encircles the finger, associated in ancient times with the heart, so it not only symbolises a pledge of eternal love but the enclosure of the heart and a pledge of fidelity[2].

The Ouroboros, a representation of coming full circle (cycle), is an ancient symbol. It depicts a serpent, or sometimes a dragon, eating its own tail, and is a symbol that most Satanists will recognise as it surrounds the Church of Satan's sigil of Baphomet. The name originates from within the Greek language; (oura) meaning "tail" and (boros) meaning "eating" and thereby simply means "he who eats the tail". The Ouroboros represents the perpetual cyclic renewal of life and infinity, the concept of eternity and the eternal return, and represents the cycle of life, death and rebirth, leading to immortality, as in the Phoenix[3].

Both the circle and the triangle are closed signs along with several others which refer to the geometric shapes to distinguish them from open signs such as the cross, arrow and spiral. Hermetic magic, for example, employs geometric shapes as functional magic paired with ritual magic which is generally used in the creation of pendants, amulets, talismans and pentacles amongst other items.

As a closed sign, the circle expands outwards to represent beginning, potential, motion, cosmos, eternity and protection. A circle within a circle indicates divinity, power, charisma, the emanation of spiritual power and the halo.

The triangle takes two basic forms normally male and female, upright it equates to the element of fire, active and masculine whereas downward it equates to the feminine or passive and the element of water. The alignment of the active and passive triangle produces the closed sign called a lozenge also referred to as a diamond.

We are obviously only interested in the upward moving triangle which is sometimes called the blade. The chalice and blade featuring ceremonially in many ritual magic operations. It is a symbol of aspiration or rising up, male force, fire as previously stated and is purely phallic in origin. The triangle represents aspiration, rising force, creation, manifestation, illumination and the male principal.

Familiar alchemy and astrology which are used in the present day were created by medieval and renaissance magicians with the most common of these being the four elements, air, water, fire and earth. In medieval times they were drawn as triangles while modern versions are drawn as circles with both the triangle and circle used in the AA symbol representing fire.

This now brings me onto the logo or sigil used on the cover of this book. Known as the philosopher's stone or the Alchemical glyph, it brings in my interest of esoterical alchemy and the idea of the philosophers stone being the 'grand magus' or great work in stripping away all the unwanted stuff from the alchemist and rebuilding them in a new form know as 'Solve et Coagula'. It also brings into play the Hermetic idea of balance, which is famously expressed by Sir Isaac Newton's translation of the Emerald Tablet: "as above, so below, as within, so without, as the universe, so the soul…"

I have incorporated the CoRS logo into the smallest circle as this is what I have used as my core foundation and structure for my own recovery. This is surrounded by a square, which symbolises 'squaring the circle' because when a circle fits into a square, it fits into the boundaries of the Laws of Nature, the four corners of the square representing the four alchemical elements and the circle contained within that representing the self.

The square also symbolises the earth, land, field, ground, foundation, security, structure, the four points of the compass and the four seasons, spring, summer, autumn and winter which further represent the waxing and waning of life.

In the Triangle that surrounds the square, you will see that I have used the Trinity to reflect the AA concept of the three most important aspects on this journey. These are Satanas, Recreatio and Cognitio; and they represent the fundamentals of my journey: Satan, Recovery and Knowledge/Wisdom.

Finally, in the outer completing circle I have included the CoRS motto of 'Satan regnat, et virtus rationi interius' – Satan reigns in reason and the power of the internal. The bottom of the circle you will also notice that I have used the Latin phrase 'Nosce te Ipsum' – know thyself. This is for me the ultimate prize of this recovery process: to fully understand yourself and be the master of your own reality and your own recovery.

[1] Frequently Asked Questions About A.A.'s History. (n.d.). Retrieved from http://www.aa.org/pages/en_US/frequently-asked- questions-about-aa-history

[2] The Secret Language of Symbols – symboldictionary.net. (n.d.). Retrieved from http://symboldictionary.net/?p=1914

[3] Ouroboros – Symbolic representation of coming full circle (cycle). (n.d.). Retrieved from http://www.crystalinks.com/ouroboros.html

Alcoholics Anonymous logo by Anamix - Own work, CC BY-SA 4.0, https://commons.wikimedia.org/w/index.php?curid=37930268

STEP 11

SOUGHT THROUGH PRAYER AND
MEDITATION TO IMPROVE OUR CONSCIOUS
CONTACT WITH GOD, AS WE UNDERSTOOD
HIM, PRAYING ONLY FOR KNOWLEDGE
OF HIS WILL FOR US AND THE POWER TO
CARRY THAT OUT.[1]

Use ritual and meditation to gain a better understanding of yourself; figure out what your goals and aims are in life; gain a focus and drive towards them.

By now you should have a good understanding of your life goals either through what you have done in the steps or by utilising the logotherapy[2] method first mentioned in the chapter 'Relapse and Power of Suggestion' and referenced in the chapter on Step 10.

In the next few chapters, I will go into more depth on the topics of magic, ritual, prayer and meditation. But for now, I would just like to point out that my styles of ritual meditation and magic are personal to me. You do not need to follow the same magical ideas. Magick is an art form, and it takes time to develop a style that suits you as an individual, so I only state it as a guide and not an absolute truth.

Another thought I will introduce here is the notion of yoga and movement as a magickal art form, the idea of movement with intent. I've never really been one for yoga if I'm honest and it took several years of persuasion from my wife to try it. That was until I discovered a style of yoga called BLACK YO)))GA. Sadly lessons are only available in the US, but they have recently produced a DVD, so I got myself a copy and found it to be very helpful, especially if I do it in a ritual type setting.

From the BLACK YO)))GA website:

> "BLACK YO)))GA is vinyasa style yoga set to drone, noise, stoner metal, ambient, industrial, space doom, and other traditional meditation music. It incorporates basic poses in a relaxed environment while focusing on safe body mechanics. It's a traditional class in practice, though darker than what you typically associate with yoga.
>
> "Our goal is to create a heavy meditative space in order to spread the benefits of

yoga to people within our own art and music communities: people who may battle with depression, anxiety, alcoholism, drug addiction, trauma/PTSD, phobias, dark passengers, etc.; those who may not feel they fit into the typical yoga classes; the people who, in all rights, may most need the balance and release of yoga to return to and lead rich, fulfilling lives."[3]

"You can't fully appreciate the light until you understand the darkness."[3]

[1] The Twelve Steps of Alcoholics Anonymous. (n.d.). Retrieved from http:// www.aa.org/assets/en_US/smf- 121_en.pdf

[2] Viktor Frankl Institute of Logotherapy. (n.d.). Retrieved from http://www. logotherapyinstitute.org/About_Logotherapy.h tml

[3] BLACK YO)))GA. (n.d.). Retrieved from http://www.black- yoga.com/

XXVII

MAGICK

Yes, I regularly spell magic with a K and this is to distinguish it from the showman's illusionary tricks that often get bracketed into the term magic. If you find this annoys you, then that's your problem, and I also don't care that LaVey said: *"Those who spell Magic with a K aren't"*.

So let's start off by attempting to define magick. Most of us that practise the art will have our own unique definitions of what magick is; some will claim it to be energy, the force of nature, a way of manipulating the universe by one's own willpower or a relationship with the spirit world. Lee Banks, the founder of the Church of Rational Satanism, actually refers to satanic magic as satanic mentalism in 'The Entombed Edition[2]' of the Rational Satanism series. He states: "we utilise many differing psychological manipulation techniques carefully selected by the individual", and goes on to say "with mentalism comes logical evaluation and rational interpretation, twisting events to your preference with completely natural techniques."

Magick itself can be split into the four paradigms of Spirit, Energy, Psychological and Information. If you want more information on what type of magic is best suited to you, then one of the Rational Satanism members has developed a simple online test (What Is Your Magical Paradigm)[3] to help you figure that out based on descriptions from Patrick Dunn's 'Postmodern Magic'[4]. I would highly recommend this book as I feel the magical techniques described in the book work really well with the rational satanic philosophy making it the best magical companion to the series I have read. As you may have deduced, I mostly fit into the Psychological Paradigm as I see reality and magic as dependent on mental perception, but I also touch on lots of other areas as well.

Magick can also be categorised into many different areas including science, art, psychology, one's own desire or will, the forces of nature, the supernatural and the four paradigms as previously mentioned. I like to think it covers all of these. The point is: if you don't allow yourself to be bogged down by following a set of rules and dogma, you can effectively make your own form of magick that complements your S-Theory and fits your rational satanic system.

The terms 'black magic' and 'white magic' are typically used to classify the type of magic that is being performed as either 'good' or 'bad'. Personally, I dislike these terms as I think it should just be magick and it is up to the person conducting the said magick to determine if it is either good or bad by their own will or intent.

I liken the art form of magick to that of art itself; some artists use oils with colours, whereas others use simple black lines. It is the skill of the artist or the magician, who works best with their tools, that will produce the greatest pieces of art and not the medium or amount of colours they are using. Therefore the type of magick you chose to use will only be as effective as you are at using it. In essence, the skill is with you the magician, not the magick.

Through my many years of doing spell craft, I have been able to look at it through the 3rd side perspective to see how these things work. This is something that comes so naturally for me that I began to question if I would lose the magick aspect by understanding the science behind what it was that I was doing. The answer I concluded was no: I could appreciate the beauty of magick while knowing its workings and this quandary is also discussed in the essay 'Don't lose the beauty'[5], an extract from the book S- Theory on the CoRS website.

I am a big fan of chaos magick and the art of sigil crafting, which I will briefly describe below.

Chaos magick employs the technique of using belief as a tool and disowning one's own 'belief' structure for a set period, which could last a few days, weeks or even months if necessary. This timeframe will allow you to completely submerge yourself in an alternative belief in order to truly believe it. This is effective in delivering change due to the strategy that you are essentially giving yourself the placebo consciously. This process can be seen in some shamanic rituals, performed by warrior tribes before battle, to get them into that invincible mind-set where they are rallied into a frenzy to intimidate the enemy and drive the fear out of their own warriors.

The approach of disowning reality for the period during ritual is how you manage to get into that psychological decompression chamber to act out your intent. I very much see the way I do magick as connecting to my understanding of psychology and through science being able to manipulate my own subconscious. This is how I imagine I am able to take my 90% and filter it through my 10% and back into the 90% for the greatest effect.

When sigil crafting you are definitively attaching your will, through a symbol, to your subconscious, for which I have had both some very good outcomes and some which have yet to produce results. Could I explain what happened in another way? Would the results still be the same had I not used magick? Maybe, maybe not, but isn't the process of performing magick part of the fun?

I told my daughter recently that I could do special magic to help her learn how to ride her bike. I told her that if we said some magic words together, an intent followed by Abracadabra (possibly derived from an Aramaic phrase meaning 'I create what I speak'), she would be able to ride the bike. We did, and within 10 minutes she was riding around without me holding on. Was that magic? To her yes, for me I can explain it away, but then it will lose the beauty and the magic!

One of the main principles, and also one of the hardest, when it comes to sigil crafting, is that once charged the intent must be forgotten in order for it to take effect. This is so the subconscious mind, rather than the conscious mind, can be brought into use to make the change happen. So in essence, if you are sitting there after you have finished a ritual, on your ritual high and you start to think: "What I did was bollocks"- it's more likely to work! (Although others may disagree on this method.)

[1] LaVey, Anton S. (1998) Satan Speaks! (Venice, CA: Feral House), p.166.

[2] Banks, Lee. (n.d.). Entombed Edition by CoRS Merchandising. CoRS, Retrieved from http://corsmerch.tictail.com/product/rational-satanism-the-entombed-edition

[3] What Is Your Magical Paradigm? (2016, August 31). Retrieved from https://www.playbuzz.com/johnpt10/what-paradigm-of- magic-do-you-perceive

[4] Dunn, P. (2005). Postmodern magic: the art of magic in the information age. St. Paul, MN: Llewellyn.

[5] Don't lose the beauty. (n.d.). Retrieved from http://www.churchofrationalsatanism.com/essays/don-t- loose-the-beauty/

XXVIII

Prayer, Ritual and Meditation

One of the things that will be suggested to you in AA is to pray. Pray in the morning for a sober day and pray at night to say thank you for a sober day. If you are anything like me, there was no way I was getting down on my knees and praying to some Christian god. I could, however, see that the symbolic nature of these two daily events could have a positive effect on my recovery. The prayer in the morning is designed to get me into that battle mode to take on the day and the prayer in the evening is to give myself that pat on the back for getting through it. I mean it wasn't that far removed from my drinking routine: a large vodka and Lucozade to get me up in the mornings and a celebratory drink, or ten, in the evening to acknowledge that I had got through another day.

I first selected a Norse verse to say to myself in the mornings, as I described in the chapter 'Archetype', but I will repeat it here as no one does battle hymns like the Vikings!

Hail Mighty Asa-Thor

I go forth today to do my duty.

I go forth today to drink deep the life
in Midgarth.

Walk beside me, great friend of man.

Lend me your strength, that I might defeat
all Jotuns in my path,

Be they giants of the world, of the mind or
of the heart

Help me do right by my kin, As you do.

Hail Thor!

I must say though I did feel like something of a tool while saying this and I would do it locked in the bathroom after brushing my teeth. It also wasn't something I did every morning; however, I did force myself to say it for quite a while, and if anything it just made me feel uncomfortable. I did, however, after a while of searching for a daily ritual, add in the selection of a rune stone to the process.

When I met with someone from the Odinist Fellowship he also had his own Odinist Serenity Prayer:

May the high ones grant me strength to
endure the things I cannot change

Thor give me courage
(to change the things I can)

Odin give me wisdom

He bellowed this out at the meeting we attended
together and drowned out most of the people there.
If it works for him that's great; personally, I found it a
bit immature.

I later changed my morning routine to include a satanic
verse taken from the Satanic Scriptures[1]:

Hail Satan full of might!
Our allegiance is with thee!

Cursed are they, the God adorers, And cursed
are the worshippers Of the Nazarene Eunuch!

Unholy Satan, bringer of enlightenment,
Lend us thy power,

Now and throughout the hours of our lives!

Shemhamforash!

I took a photo of this section in the book, so I could
read it to myself on my short walk to work. I would
then listen to a song I had picked out for myself to
get me in the right mood for the day. When I got to
work on my tea break, I would generally look up the
rune that I had picked out that morning and use it as a
reflection for the day.

I later fizzled out the morning prayers and just went for a good old blast of heavy metal as I found it had the same effect for me. If you find saying "give us this day our satanic bread...", screaming blasphemies or listening to classical music works better for you then do it, when it comes to the finish it's your recovery, not mine. You have to find what works for you, not anyone else, so don't be put off doing something that works for you if someone else tells you it didn't work for them.

Meditation and ritual were something else I found useful in my recovery system. I used both in very similar ways by using the 90% 10% Thinking[2] process. I use magic in the same process and that is discussed in more detail elsewhere in the book.

90% 10% Thinking[2] is one of the core foundations of the Rational Satanism philosophy. I found it allows me to take rational thoughts from my 90% to an irrational part of my thinking or my 10% fraction where they can be manipulated.

Learning to pay attention to our feelings and inclinations without engaging them is probably the most powerful tool in treating addiction. These claims are supported by several studies done over the past dozen years, which show that the brain actually undergoes changes, both temporary (during the time of meditation) and permanent. Additionally, one recent study showed that the amygdalas, (areas deep in each hemisphere of the brain, which are associated with stress, strong emotional responses and memory) of participants shrunk significantly, over just eight weeks, as they engaged regularly in a set of three meditative and mindful exercises. Although these people were chosen for the studies based on stress levels, rather than anything associated with addiction, the fact that they were able to physically change their brains through conscious practice shows that it is possible to have an effect.

One of the first things I had done utilising my 10% (irrational part of the brain) before I was even aware of the concept, was a candle meditation to remove negative thoughts. It's really simple to do, and you can try it on your own without much guidance. I was fully aware of the science behind what I was doing, and I will explain this at the end.

THE CANDLE MEDITATION/RITUAL

Sit in a dark room, with as little about as possible to limit distractions. Make sure you are comfortable as you could be sitting there for about half an hour or so.

Light a candle and stare into the flame (candle colour is up to you). I use music to help block out outside distractions, you can use headphones if you want too, I find drone or doom works best – I normally go for Monoliths & Dimensions by Sunn O))) and play it really loud! If you want to use incense to add to the atmosphere by all means do but pick something that you like or feel a connection too! (The science will tell you why later!)

Focus your negative energy going into the flame and disappearing with the smoke. Then think of positive outcomes for situations that have already happened in your life and absorb them like the light from the flame. Think about how they make you feel. Your eyes focus should constantly be on the flame. (You may see two or three flames at some point; this is normal.) If you want to say stuff then you can, if you feel like moving do it. Just keep your focus on the flame.

Focus on your breathing and make sure it's calm and relaxed, close your eyes and try to visualise the candle and think of the positive feeling you absorbed from the candle. When you open your eyes, stare back at the candle and do the same again. Continue doing this until you have a good mental image of the candle.

If you feel you can't properly visualise it, take a picture with your phone. Sit with the candle for as long as you like after

When you are done, if you feel like you want to laugh, do it; if you feel stupid, that's good.

Your eyes will probably hurt when you turn your lights back on. (I looked stoned!)

HOW IT WORKS

Now get on with your normal life; when you feel the negativity coming into you thought process visualise the candle, or look at the picture on your phone if you are finding it hard to imagine the candle. You should see the negative thoughts disappear and be replaced with the positive ones you focused on.

The basic science behind this is a mind association process. You have given your positive experiences an image: the candle. You can now recall that image in your daily life to help you remove negative thought processes. If you have used incense, you should be able to do the same thing with the smell. This phenomenon is odd for me now as I get smell sensations when I have memory triggers!

I know full well in my 90% (rational part of the brain) that everything I do in that 10% (irrational part of the brain) is a trick I play on myself. It's the decompression from reality that allows for the psychic change that I want to achieve. For me, it works especially well when I need to get something pushed forward. You see the 10% is an act, a ploy to get as close to your godhead and your core self as you can.

Another great method to use for a daily ritual is the laughter banishing technique. This is where you simply laugh off any thoughts of drinking that might come into your mind. If you look at demonology, you'll find that most demons will attach themselves to and work on your fears. The best approach is to laugh them away; fear can't take a hold if you are laughing in its face!

Frequently you will hear a lot of talk in AA about 'letting go'. For this, I put the symbolic aspect of ritual to good use by writing down what I want to let go on a piece of paper and then either setting fire to it (in a controlled way), attaching it to a helium balloon or burying it in the ground. Ideas and thoughts are difficult to remove, but with this method, once it's gone, it's gone, and you can see it going. Much in the same way, a goat was traditionally used to symbolically take on all the sins of a village and then be led out to be sacrificed, leaving all in the village free from sin and coining the term scapegoat.

Finally, I think we'll round this chapter off with some comments on Altars as they are, of course, the big show piece. You will come across many opinions on these, what to have, where to put it and so on and so forth; so I will only give you my opinion, and it is for you to find out what you feel is best for you if, indeed, you want one at all.

My altar space fits into an artists' travel box. This box case contains all the basic equipment I need to set up a ritual space wherever I am, inside or out. I will make sure the set up of my altar is part of the ritual process, and I feel this also adds to the symbolic nature of where everything is placed and allows me the time to get into the correct mind space. Then, when I am done, things are tidied back into the box. This enables me to visually see when I am using my 10% (irrational part of the brain) and also facilitates my journey both into and out of the ritual.

By doing things this way it also makes it a great space saver; stops things gathering dust. I also don't need to worry about the kids playing with stuff they shouldn't, and it also avoids the odd questions from visitors to my home. (However, I can see how some would find this a good conversation starter.)

[1] Gilmore, P. H. (2007). The Satanic Scriptures. Baltimore, MD: Scapegoat. Retrieved from https://archive.org/stream/TheSatanicScriptures/The%20S atanic%20Scriptures_djvu.txt

[2] 90% 10% Thinking. (n.d.). Retrieved from http://www. churchofrationalsatanism.com/essays/90-10- thinking/

[3] Addicts are NOT Powerless – LifeRing. (n.d.). Retrieved from http://lifering. org/addicts-are-not-powerless/

STEP 12

**HAVING HAD A SPIRITUAL AWAKENING AS THE
RESULT OF THESE STEPS, WE TRIED TO CARRY THIS
MESSAGE TO ALCOHOLICS, AND TO PRACTICE
THESE PRINCIPLES IN ALL OUR AFFAIRS.[1]**

Use your voice to loudly and proudly say: I am a
Satanist and I used these steps to get sober without
your Christian God – and carry this message to other
people seeking help in the fellowship who struggle
with the monotheistic middle eastern death cult[2]
concept of 'God'.

This is where you truly stand with horns for everyone
to see as...

Satan (Hebrew: שָׂטָן satan, meaning "enemy" or
"adversary";

This is where you give hope to those that have been told by militant pro-god AA members and militant Anti-AA warriors that you do not need God for this programme and you are living proof. I find both the pro and anti-AA squads as bad as each other, as they both offer the same thing: an easy excuse for people to go out and use again.

For many, AA and the 12 step programme is the most accessible programme of recovery from any addiction and so working with your perception of it, to help you and others to recover, will give the largest number of people the chance to follow you in conquering their addictions.

The AA system is not perfect, and neither is any other system of recovery because that is the danger of having a written scripture. It literally sets in stone something that should be allowed to change, grow and evolve with the individual. Unless you are willing to adapt yourself and add concepts to what is 'set in stone', in whatever recovery programme you choose, the likelihood of success is limited. Therefore, I believe your chances are vastly improved by making your own recovery S-Theory, 'Paradigm Shifting' to walk through the 'Gates of Hell' and finding out what works best for you as an individual.

Then you will become Lucifer, bringing the light of hope for those that had thought that they were destined to float in and out of recovery and using until they died.

I also feel it is at this point that we should be trying to inject some change into the programme. In particular, we should attempt to get the chapter "we agnostics" either modified or removed from the AA big book as I and many I have spoken to, find it misleading and belittling of anyone who has overcome their addiction using this programme without 'god'. The only way we will be able to do this is, en masse, all together as members of the AA fellowship through our own intergroups to the main AA head office.

Step 12, in my opinion, is what provides encouragement to create the militant ideas from both the pro and anti-AA camps and results in people questioning: "Am I really a true alcoholic or addict?". This question is normally met with the response: "Well go and try for yourself, perform an experiment, see if you can drink like a normal person and then come back and tell us how you got on if you make it back." Well, if you are like me, you will have countless examples of these very experiments. They will be written down so that you can reference them, thanks to your Step 4 and 5 work. And you'll be able to say: "Yes, looking at the evidence I have gathered from my previous 'experiments', I am able to hypothesise the outcome if I was to attempt to drink and use again. Thus, I have concluded that I am indeed an addict or alcoholic and I do not need to prove that to anyone other than myself. I am my own god and master of my own reality, and I have the evidence to prove it."

---

[1] The Twelve Steps of Alcoholics Anonymous. (n.d.). Retrieved from http://www.aa.org/assets/en_US/smf- 121_en.pdf

[2] Baddeley, G. (2016). Lucifer rising. London: Plexus Publishing Limited.

XXIX

13

Originally I was going to call this book "The 13th Step – a Rational Satanic Recovery". I did some research into the number 13, and it fitted perfectly with the system. Then I looked into the 13th step and found that it already is a well- known term within AA and not for very good reasons either. It turns out that '13th stepping' is a term used for men (mostly) who 12 step women all the way into bed. Because I didn't want this book to be associated with that movement, it has the title that is on the cover now. However, just because of the context used by AA I didn't want you to miss out on the research, so I have kept it in for you to enjoy.

The folklore and almost legendary aspects of the number 13 have been noted in various cultures around the world where they are strikingly similar. One of the main theories that surround the number is that this is due to many cultures employing lunar-solar calendars.[1]

Mathematically there are approximately 12.41 lunations or full moons per solar year, and hence 12 "true months" plus a smaller and often portentous thirteenth month. A year with 13 full moons instead of 12 posed problems for the monks in charge of the calendars as not only was it considered a very unfortunate circumstance, especially by the monks who had charge of the calendar of thirteen months for that year, but it also upset the regular arrangement of church festivals.

Ancient cultures also used the number 13 to represent femininity because it corresponded to the number of lunar or menstrual cycles in a year ($13 \times 28 = 364$ days). The theory is that, as the solar calendar triumphed over the lunar, the number thirteen became anathema and stigmatised.

According to Varg Vikernes in the book Sorcery and Religion in Ancient Scandinavia[2]:

> "The Scandinavian Bronze Age calender, known from a rock carving of a woman, found in what is today known as Bohuslan (in Sweden), has 13 months, each with exactly 28 days. There was also a new year's day that every leap year lasted for two days, so all in all, it has 365 days (and 366 every leap year) too. This is, in fact, the most accurate calendar known from the ancient world."

He further goes on to talk about the days of the week, stating that Sundays were the start of the week. However, I would like to draw your attention to Friday.

> "The Friday was the day of love, and naturally the day of the goddess of love. The second Friday of every month was the Friday of the week of birth and was, therefore, seen as a particularly favourable day for marriage. This Friday, the 13th day of every month, was also seen as the birth of the deity. All the thirteen most important deities' birthdays were celebrated in turn, one every month of the year, and every year."

I find this a very significant point and one that explains the stigma around the date Friday the 13th. It would have been seen by some, I'm sure, as a date where the solar and lunar calendars crossed over or married up. Therefore, for the many pagans oppressed by Christianity all across Europe, this would have been a day to remember and celebrate their old gods, which would have been deemed a heretical and blasphemous act at the time.

13 is not just stigmatised or worshipped in Christianity and pagan religions, so it's also helpful to see where else it fits in other cultures. One of which was a Sikh religion. According to famous Sakhi or the story of Guru Nanak Dev Ji, when he was an accountant at a town of Sultanpur Lodhi, he was distributing groceries to people. When he gave groceries to the 13th person,

he stopped because in Gurmukhi and Hindi the word 13 is called Terah, which means yours. And Guru Nanak Dev Ji kept saying, "Yours, yours, yours…"[1]

This story was one of the many reasons 13 resonated with me as a title number for this book as it's your recovery and it's yours to own. But let's look at some of the other stories behind the number 13 now both on the positive and negative spectrum. You will also notice there are lots of times where it can be linked to the idea of recovery.

The Aztecs, for example, considered thirteen to be a very sacred number. It was the number of time and stood for completion as the Aztec week lasted for thirteen days.

The Aztec year was 260 days, which was divided into 20 thirteen-day periods. The 13- day period is called a Trecena, and in Aztec mythology, the goddess Tlazolteotl ruled the 13th Trecena. She was the goddess of sin and a patroness of adulterers. She could also forgive sins, especially those of a sexual nature. Tlazolteotl is associated with purifying steam baths.

13 is the number of the Tarot card 'Death'. Death symbolises getting rid of the old and making room for something new. It's a tarot card about transformation where reversed it signifies a failure to move on to something better. These are, of course, very basic interpretations, and those of you that have worked with your own tarot sets will have a much deeper personal understanding of this card in the deck.

The 13th Runic letter is the Eihwaz which is associated with Yggdrasil, the Tree of Life.

In the Bible the 13th year was the year of rebellion; "Twelve years they had served Chedor-lao'mer, but in the thirteenth year they rebelled." *Genesis 14:4*

King Solomon spent 13 years building his own house (palace) before it was finished.[1] *King 7:1*

13 Links into Christianity in several other areas as well. The Last Supper: At Jesus Christ's last supper, there were thirteen people around the table, counting Christ and the twelve apostles. Some believe this is unlucky because one of those thirteen, Judas Iscariot, was the betrayer of Jesus Christ.[1]

However, others see it as a divine number as it represents the twelve apostles and Jesus, with Jesus being the 13th member. To this day though, it is still considered unlucky to have 13 guests at a dinner party, unless you were part of the 'Hellfire Club', of course, originating in the 18th century where it was the norm.

On Friday 13th October 1307, King Philip IV of France ordered the arrest of the Knights Templar and most of the knights were tortured and burnt alive for being part of a 'Devil Worshiping Cult'.

The key tenets of alchemy are found in something called the emerald tablet, which is a text said to reveal the secret of the primordial substance and its transmutation. The text contains 13 lines including the well-known Hermetic axiom "as above, so below" as translated by Sir Isaac Newton.

And finally we'll end on this, the baker's dozen also known as the devil's dozen, long dozen, or long measure is 13, which is one more than a standard dozen (12). This practice came about because bakers would be fined if they gave any less than 12 full weight loaves so they would always give 13 just to be on the safe side.

As you can see, there was a lot linking the number 13 both to the process of the 12 step recovery programme and Satanism, but I hope you like the title I went for in the end.

[1] 13 (number) – Wikipedia. (n.d.). Retrieved fromhttps://en.wikipedia.org/wiki/13_(number)

[2] Vikernes, V. (2011). Sorcery and religion in ancient Scandinavia. London: Abstract Sounds Books.

XXX

SATANIC MIND FOOD FOR THOSE IN RECOVERY

During my recovery, I would pick up phrases that were useful to me. I even made some up myself. Mine are the ones not in "quotes". I hope you find them useful.

"Forgive and forget" from a magical perspective: If we do not allow negative emotions and thoughts to manifest, then we are not giving power to them. This is, in essence, forgiving where they came from. If we don't allow the negative thoughts brain space, then we forget about them. As a comforting thought, those negative emotions have no choice but to return to their original source as they will have no power over you.

> "The inspiration you seek is already within you. Be silent and listen"
> – *Rumi*

Do not allow someone to get into your head! Some would perceive this as turning the other cheek, but I would consider not reacting or rising to someone, who wants a reaction, the best way to smash them back in the face. Sometimes the best course of action is the course of non-action.

> "It's all about falling in love with yourself and sharing that love with someone who appreciates you, rather than looking to compensate for a self love deficit"
> – *Eartha Kitt*

People, places and things only have power if you give it to them and that includes you.

> "Each man creates his own god for himself – his own heaven, his own hell"
> *The Masque of the Red Death (1964 film)*

Self-will run riot is a false statement.

It's trying to force your will onto others unsuccessfully that causes you problems. However many still try to use this form of manipulation by exchanging the word 'self-will' with God.

By accepting a god in recovery, you are merely changing your master rather than ceasing to be a slave.

> "Stop blindly following the words of the book and look at the situation. You have completed your training, but you must now learn to apply it. Regurgitation is not the answer, simple analysis and thought must be used to solve the problem"
>
> *Warhammer 40K Quotes*

As a drinker, I tried to please everyone but myself, to be things I wasn't. I used drink to try to feel accepted and drown my feelings of confliction within myself. So by accepting a god, who is not me, I am no better off than I was before.

'Handing your will over to god' is just a way of diverting your attention and allowing you to change your focus. The technique allows you not to concentrate on the small things you may want to change, but instead look at the big picture, in order to 'paradigm shift' and cause a fundamental change of perspective to occur. Based on this knowledge, you do not need 'god' to do this for you; you can do it yourself.

Living word for word by a book published in 1939 and backing it up with a work of fiction, mistranslated from the original sources over centuries, is utter stupidity. The AA big book should be used as a tool and not worshipped as a religious text.

If I want to manipulate people to do my will I don't feel I should have to hide behind a god like a shield to do so.

> "When we thank god for our success, we don't take credit, when we blame him for our failures we don't take responsibilities"
>
> *– Unknown*

> "Everything that irritates us about others can lead us to an understanding of ourselves"
>
> *– Carl Jung*

Just because we feel emotions, this does not mean we are very good at expressing them.

> "I search for god and found only myself. I searched for myself and found only god"
>
> *– Rumi*

XXXI

FURTHER DOWN THE RABBIT HOLE...

...we tumble. Here is a list of books that I would suggest for further reading. Some of these books you may have already read, some of them may be completely new to you. These are some of the books that I have personally read, am currently in the process of reading or working my way through those that have been suggested to me, either way, they all sit on my bookshelf should I need them.

I have tried to break them down into different subject areas should you wish to look further into some subjects more than others. Remember these are just suggested books from my own personal recovery system; you may find some not helpful at all and you will most certainly want to add your own.

SATANISM:

The full **Rational Satanism** collection – I would especially recommend **Futureproof Adaptability** and **S-Theory**

Satanic Health, Mental Wealth by C.M. Wulver

Satanic Bible by Anton LaVey

Satanic Rituals by Anton LaVey

Devil's Notebook by Anton LaVey

Satanic Scriptures by Peter H Gilmore

Lucifer Rising: A Book of Sin, Devil Worship and Rock'n'roll by Gavin Baddeley

Satanic Collections by Michael Sartin

Paradise Lost by John Milton

The Inferno (Divine Comedy) by Dante

The Satanic Witch by Anton LaVey
(men, you really should read this book)

LUCIFER: princeps by Peter Grey

MAGIC AND THE OCCULT:

Postmodern Magic by Patrick Dunn

Condensed Chaos by Phil Hine

Liber Null & Psychonaut by Peter J Carroll

Practical Sigil Magic by Frater U∴D∴

Real Alchemy by Robert Allen Bartlett

Magick: Book 4 by Aleister Crowley

The Book of Pleasure by Austin Osman Spare

The Gentle Arts of Nature Magic by
Marian Green

The Witches Bible by Janet and Stewart Farrar

Apocalyptic Witchcraft by Peter Grey

The Goetia – The Lesser Key of Solomon the King by Mathers/Crowley

Sigils, Ciphers and Scripts – History and Graphic Function of Magick Symbols by M.B. Jackson

ADDICTION:

Rational Recovery by Jack Trimpey

Under the Influence: a guide to the myths and realities of alcoholism by James R. Milam, Ph.D., and Katherine Ketcham

Alcoholics Anonymous (the Big Book)

Chasing the Scream by Johann Hari

OTHER AREAS OF INTEREST:

Runes – Theory and Practice by Galina Krasskova

Sorcery and Religion in Ancient Scandinavia by Varg Vikernes

Shamanism and the Psychology of C.G.Jung by Robert E. Ryan

Chaos: Making a New Science by James Gleick

The book of Enoch by R. H. Charles

Pooh and the Philosophers by John Tyerman Willams

Beyond Good and Evil by Friedrich Nietzsche

Might is Right by Ragnar Redbeard

There are a few people, however, that I may have missed off the books list, as I don't own any copies of their work, but feel they are worthy of note, so I will add them here so that you can look them up as well:

Joseph John Campbell, Ayn Rand, Carl G Jung, Eliphas Levi

There are, of course, areas that I might have missed, but this will give you a quite a bit to sink your teeth into when you feel the need to expand your own ideas. I also think it goes to show that to develop the best system for your recovery you cannot limit yourself to one book or one idea.

Acknowledgements

First of all, I would like to thank John Wait and Lee Banks for their encouragement and patience while I undertook this project.

I'd like to further extend my thanks to Lee who has helped to get the first edition of this book published through CoRS Publishing.

Additional thanks go to my friends Alex Piglowski for his help with the logo I designed, Rob Brightwell for his help and advice with the website and Jon Sturdy, aka bio dad, for his expert photographic skills.

Thanks must also go to my long suffering wife, Audrey, who has had to deal with me for the last 14 years and her patience and understanding from the end of my drinking through my recovery and while I completed this project (now for the second time!).

My extended thanks and gratitude goes to Mark Dean, aka Dad, for his tireless efforts with proofreading and editing. He is one of the reasons the book is in its current form. Any remaining mistakes are mine (edited). I apologise for my exceptionally long sentences and 'overuse' of the word twat!!

Finally and by no means least, Esther Lemmens at Zesty Books for her amazing attention to detail and wonderful eye for style in making this second edition what it is now.

ABOUT BEN

Ben was born in Greenwich, London, UK.

His first memory of drinking was on a school ski trip where, aged 11, after a full crate of beer, a shy boy became the life of the party! Reaching his teens, blacking out became a regular occurrence while out with his friends. A first year at university – away from home – unleashed a new level of substance misuse and he experimented with several different drugs including speed, cocaine, magic mushrooms and ecstasy. He would end up in hospital on multiple occasions with varying degrees of injuries.

After an - unsurprisingly - unsuccessful year at university, Ben started working with friends in the music industry and this constant interaction with 'weekend rock stars' entrenched his drinking and drug use.

At the end of a touring season, Ben met his wife. He was so drunk that he doesn't actually remember their first kiss which embarrasses him to this day. Leaving the music circle behind him, he started as a trainee groundsman in a school and enjoyed it enough to try and curb his drinking. This did not come easy! After a night out that he cannot remember and an early morning argument, Ben sank two shots of absinthe and went on the train to work. He got there, but turned around, phoned in sick and went drinking. After a 10 hour blackout and nearly losing his relationship with his now wife, he decided he needed to look for other options. This was his pivotal moment. After a few days of detoxing at home he went to his first AA meeting on November 1st 2007, aged just 24. This was however only the beginning of a new struggle to find a recovery system that suited him and take on his journey of self-analysis, acceptance and recovery.

After exploring different strands of religion, spirituality and philosophy, Ben became a member of the Church of Rational Satanism (CoRS) in 2015 before becoming a chairman. He regularly writes online, has led a series of talks at UK universities on the subject of Satanism, and is a proud volunteer at the Human Library (and would encourage everyone to attend one of their events where reading a Human Book will dispel myths and prejudices about your fellow human beings.)

PASS THROUGH THE 9TH GATE

I reject all the biblical views of the truth

Dismiss it as the folklore of the times

I won't be force fed prophecies

From a book of untruths for the weakest mind

I keep the bible in a pool of blood

So that none of its lies can affect me

Slayer, New Faith
(from the album *God Hates Us All*)

Lightning Source UK Ltd.
Milton Keynes UK
UKHW020858210319
339577UK00002B/26/P